Th Gospel of Thomas

The *Enlightenment* Teachings

of *Jesus*

Karina Library Press
Ojai, California
2010

Karina Library
PO Box 35
Ojai, California 93024
805.500.4535

www.karinalibrary.com
discover@karinalibrary.com

The Gospel of Thomas: The Enlightenment Teachings of Jesus
ISBN-13: 978-0-9824491-2-7

www.enlightenedjesus.com
www.livingnonduality.org

Available in Kindle and iBookstore editions.

The publication of this manuscript made possible through the assistance of Rev. Theddius Leitho of Florida, an acquaintance of the nondual teachings for many years.

Also by Robert Wolfe

Living Nonduality: Enlightenment Teachings of Self-Realization

TABLE OF CONTENTS

Depending upon the reader's degree of interest in the subject, there are varied ways in which the material in this book can be accessed.

It is intended to be read in the order in which it is presented. Some, however, might prefer to first read the section where all of the Gospel of Thomas verses have been commented on in the context of their teachings as representing the nondual enlightenment perspective. (Commentary on Verses: Nondual Perspective).

But in order to fully *know* the Gospel of Thomas, there are many important elements to know *about* the Gospel of Thomas; and for that purpose the material preceding the verse-commentary section (Text: The "Fifth" Gospel) needs to be read as well.

Whatever the choice, some readers might find it useful to have as an accompanying resource a copy of the English translation of the Gospel of Thomas in which all the verses are given in numerical order. The recommended translation is that of Thomas O. Lambdin, which can be found online by searching for "The Gospel of Thomas Translation of Thomas O. Lambdin." This translation is also available in *The Nag Hammadi Library in English*, edited by James Robinson (Harper-Collins, San Francisco; 1990).

The reader might also find it useful to have on hand a reference copy of the *New Testament*, particularly the New International Version.

These suggested references are not necessary for the reading, however, since the text was written to be understood on its own.

Although a number of New Testament scholars and biblical translators are quoted, no bibliography is included here; with today's access to Google and Wikipedia, authors' publications can readily be located.

Scholars, over time, have quoted from evolving translations of the Gospel of Thomas, so this accounts for variance in some of the wordings they cite.

They also occasionally use different titles when referring to apocryphal texts, since these reference titles too have evolved with subsequent translations. The title which each particular scholar prefers is the one which is cited here.

The quotations from the scholars, given here, are not always in the order in which they appear in the resource material; they are sometimes reordered so as to more directly reach the point in the discussion. And extraneous text, in quotations, is often abridged, due to the quantity of material included here.

Additionally, particular words are italicized for emphasis, including some in the source quotations.

It should be understood that not all of the scholarly sources, quoted here, agree entirely with the premises of this presentation. And probably there is not one of them who would agree with all the premises.

ACKNOWLEDGEMENTS: FACT-FINDERS ALL

As noted in the Appendix:

> In recent times, within the past fifty to a hundred years, discoveries have begun to cast an intensifying light on the historical facts of Jesus' life and era. And the reason *why* the New Testament authors made their varying claims—and why these particular accounts were chosen to be represented as the "gospel truth"—has become discomfortingly clear.

The spiritual and religious world owes an unending debt of gratitude to the unsung scholars, across many professional disciplines and from varied parts of the world, who have committed their careers to the serious study and reconstruction of the scriptural reports concerning the controversial figure known as Jesus.

Probably the majority of scholars who have undertaken the task of discerning what Jesus *really* did and *really* taught, did so willingly at risk that their own preconceptions—based upon their variety of religious upbringing—might be forced to be abandoned.

But, fortunately for us who benefit from their historical discoveries, the preponderance of these researchers have held the factual truth to be of greater value to society at large than would the maintenance of fabricated legends and stultifying theology.

As the inspiration for their scholarship evidently trusted in his own life: "The truth shall set us free."

AUTHOR'S NOTE: LOOKING ANEW

This treatise concerning *The Gospel of Thomas* was not originally intended to be a book-length manuscript.

Over the years, I have casually collected material from a myriad of sources that elucidated what can be known of what is called the "historical Jesus". My interest in the facts of Jesus' life (and the authenticity of his pronouncements) long predated my introduction to the non-Christian scriptures of the East, such as Buddhism, Taoism, and Advaita. After all, I was raised (and baptized at 13) as a Baptist. When I first came across a translation of *The Gospel of Thomas*, I wanted to determine how that testament of Jesus' "unknown" sayings contributed to the overall picture of who Jesus was, and what he had taught.

A friend, a (now deceased) professor who retired to Australia, asked me to write for him—from that unorganized file I had collected—what *to me* appeared to be the answer to the question of how *The Gospel of Thomas* informed our understanding of the historical Jesus and his message.

Originally I wrote only the section "Commentary on Verses" that is listed here in the Table of Contents, which give my annotation on each aphorism in Thomas. The next question followed though: If these are *authentic* sayings of Jesus, why were they not in public circulation until 1945?

And another significant question needed to be answered: Why would anyone conclude that they *are* authentic scriptures? These questions led to writing"The Fifth Gospel" material.

The value of my compilation, I feel, is that it may be of service in drawing attention to the importance of not relegating the "gnostic" Jesus to a dismissive category. There's something of invaluable significance that's been overlooked, so far, in the academic and scholarly biblical discussion. That's why this manuscript was composed.

You have eyes,
        but you do not see;
you have ears,
        but you do not hear.

(One quotation of Jesus that all four
New Testament gospels agree on.)

Peasants digging at the base of a cliff along the Nile River, in 1945, unearthed a tall, sealed clay jar that had been secreted beneath a boulder. The site of the discovery—near the village of Nag Hammadi in Upper Egypt, about 200 miles south of Cairo—is three miles from what had been the ancient Christian monastery of St. Pachomius, founded in the 4th Century.

The jar, when broken open, held thirteen leather-bound volumes, or codices, which contained 52 tractates, now collectively known as the Nag Hammadi Library.

The writing on the papyrus tractates was in Coptic, an ancient Egyptian language (still used in rituals of the Coptic Church in Egypt and Ethiopia).

In 1978, the first complete English translation was published as *The Nag Hammadi Library*, edited by James Robinson of Claremont Graduate School—"an enormous influence on the study of early Christianity," as one scholar has remarked on the volume.

As long ago as 1985, there were already 397 treatises that had been published on one of the tractates alone—the Gospel of Thomas, which has now come to be known among New Testament scholars as "The Fifth Gospel".

Here are a few of the phrases that some of the New Testament experts have used to describe the discovery of this text:

"An influential and provocative source in discussions of the historical Jesus and early interpretations of Jesus."

"The single most important non-canonical book yet to be uncovered."

"A very important discovery...probably doing more as a single text to advance our understanding of the historical Jesus (and of the transmission of his teachings) than all the Dead Sea Scrolls put together."

"Any discussion of the history of the synoptic tradition today must take into account the newly discovered Coptic gospel of Thomas, for here we have a gospel radically different from the synoptic gospels."

"No composition from Nag Hammadi has generated more excitement or controversy than the Coptic Gospel of Thomas."

"One of the most important archaeological finds in the history of New Testament scholarship...every bit as revolutionary for the study of the New Testament as the Dead Sea Scrolls are for the study of the Hebrew bible...an entirely independent 'sayings' gospel."

"The most important part of the [Nag Hammadi] library for understanding the historical Jesus..."

"A gospel that understands 'salvation' to come from some other means than a 'risen' Jesus."

"Could this new gospel fill in some of the gaps left by the canonical portrayals of Jesus, his life, his preaching?"

◎

Unlike most of the other documents in the Library, the Gospel of Thomas is a complete volume in its entirety, although (like the others) there are some words that are missing occasionally among the sentences: surmised substitutions are usually indicated by parentheses in the translation.

The composition presents (what have been numbered as) 114 "sayings" or teachings that are attributed directly to Jesus, recorded in what appears to be a random pattern.

A list of what the Gospel of Thomas is *not* will indicate how different it is from all other scriptures (including those in the Library):

- *It has no chronological narrative; no biographical detail, such as a birth scene; no account of a ritual with John the Baptist.*

- *There are no miracles; no crowds of followers; no temple confrontations.*

- *No crucifixion or resurrection tales; no theology of sin, judgment, hell or redemption.*

- *No misogyny (Salome and Mary are two of the five disciples named); no discussion of founding a church; no talk of a Second Coming; and no pious rephrasing of Old Testament commandments.*

"Thomas," of course, was the name (according to all four New Testament gospels and the book of Acts) of one of the twelve in Jesus' inner circle.

According to an anecdote in the gospel of John (11:7-16), Jesus said at one point that he intended once again to "go back to Judea."

"You are going back there," disciples queried, where "the Jews tried to stone you?!"

Jesus was firm: "I am going there."

"Then Thomas said to the rest of the disciples, 'Let us also go, that we may die with him.'"

Also, according to early Christian tradition (*tradition*, to scholars, means "account passed from generation to generation"), Thomas was alleged to have traveled to India to spread Jesus' teachings. This is now believed to be a legend.

However, the true authors of even the four New Testament gospels are entirely unknown. The names of "apostles" were ascribed to each of the Bible's gospels many decades after they were composed, and this is evidently true in the attribution of the Gospel of Thomas as well.

One of the scholars who has diligently studied the Nag Hammadi texts is Elaine Pagels, who is a Professor of Religion at Princeton University. She received her doctorate from Harvard University, and chaired the Department of Religion at Barnard College. She authored *The Gnostic Gospels*, which received several prestigious book awards after its 1979 publication.

She says:

"Some scholars have observed that whoever assembled the sayings that constitute the Gospel of Thomas may have been less an author than a compiler—or several compilers—who, rather than *composing* these sayings, simply *collected* traditional sayings and wrote them down."

It is possible that the reason why Thomas' name is appended to this particular text is that he is the one, of five disciples named, who appears to have comprehended Jesus' message.

In any event, just as with the four New Testament gospels, scholars refer to this one as *Thomas* in the same manner they refer to—although anonymously-written—*Matthew, Mark, Luke* and *John*.

Bound into the same volume with Thomas was another treatise titled after a Jesus disciple, the *Gospel of Philip*.

Pagels says of this material:

"Other sayings in this collection criticize common Christian beliefs, such as the virgin birth or the bodily resurrection, as naive misunderstandings. Bound together with these gospels is the *Apocryphon* (literally, 'secret book') *of John*, which opens with an offer to reveal 'the mysteries [and the] things hidden in silence' which Jesus taught to his disciple John."

To anyone who is thoroughly acquainted with the sagacious teachings of *nonduality*, the sayings of the Gospel of Thomas, as a body (and *whether* or *not* they can actually be attributed to Jesus of Nazareth) stand out as a representation of this venerable perspective.

As perhaps the first presentation of spiritual teachings to have appeared in a written language (Sanskrit), the ancient texts known as the Vedas (*veda* means "knowledge") formed the foundation of what is known as *advaita*, the perspective of "self-realization" as revealed through insight into nonduality.

Generally known as "enlightenment" teachings, once most prominent in the culture of India, they gained attention in a wide periphery of the East following the lifetime of the Buddha ("the enlightened one") around 500 B.C.E.*

Down to the present period, there have been renowned exponents of the teachings of nonduality, such as Ramana Maharshi in southern India, who died as recently as 1950. And there are many popular present-day teachers of nonduality in various parts of the world.

Thus, it is perplexing that of the many books that have been written to analyze the content of Thomas, it seems that no connection has been noticed regarding its nondual perspective.

Apparently, there are a couple of reasons for this. Few people, relatively, in the Western world are truly conversant with the spiritual teachings that predominate in the East. Couple that with the fact that virtually all of the translators and analysts of Thomas have been members of the religious faculty of universities in North America and Europe, who generally spend their entire career focused on Judeo-Christian studies mainly concerning the Old and the New Testament.

---

* B.C. (Before Christ) and A.D. (Anno Domini, in the year of the Lord) have in modern times been updated to B.C.E. (Before the Common Era) and C.E. (Common Era). Generally the usage in the text will follow the quote referenced.

A reader of their interpretations of the verses in Thomas can frequently notice in the scholars' phraseology that Jesus and Christianity are synonymous in their minds. The late Norman Perrin, Associate Professor of New Testament at the University of Chicago's Divinity School, has written about this assumption that every reference to *Jesus* is a reference to the *Christ* as the Church has fashioned him:

> "Again, most serious research into the teaching of Jesus is carried on by historians who are also Christians, and who, therefore, by definition have some concept of the 'risen Lord' of their faith and experience, and of his teachings to them. This naturally, even unconsciously, influences them, and can lead to the situation where a historian carefully disentangles the original Jesus-of-history from the Christ-of-faith (of the first-century Church) only to re-identify him with the Christ of his own faith, and so reinterpret the teaching all over again."

In addition, there has formed an understanding of a branch of theological doctrine (that historically appears to have been competitive with nascent Christianity) which scholars now term Gnosticism. Because many of the tractates in the Library have been classified as gnostic, the assumption seems to be that Thomas falls into this category. This uninsightful preconception hinders the consideration of Thomas as a unique viewpoint—one of which perhaps makes it most surely that of the incomparable Jesus.

This parochial tunnel vision is surprising when one considers that even contemporary Catholic theologians, such as Thomas Merton and Father Thomas Keating, have been able to explicate the nondual underpinnings that they feel can be beneficially studied in Taoist and Buddhist scriptures.

15

Some examples, of how Christian conditioning (or preoccupation concerning "Gnosticism") plays into the interpretations of various scholars, follow. (Since there is no intention here to denigrate these scholars, their names will be omitted.)

One (who frequently refers to Jesus as "the Saviour," although he is never called that in the Gospel of Thomas) claims that the Thomas verse 92—in which Jesus does not say one word about passing on knowledge about "the *heavenly* world"—would have to have been a verse spoken by "the *Risen* Lord," because: "Not until after the Resurrection can he pass on knowledge about the heavenly world."

He also opines of verse 61:

> "Salome is evidently inquiring here after Jesus' true nature. She is bewildered that this Jesus, who sat down on her bench, who ate, and who appeared as a man in every respect, can have any pretensions to being a Saviour."

There is no mention of the word *Saviour* anywhere in the verse. Moreover, there is nothing to suggest that Jesus is pretending anything, in any sense; nor that Salome is bewildered about his doing so. All of the statements of Jesus are expository, and his answer to her question ("Who are you?") is followed by her capitulation, making her "your disciple."

In another example, disrobing—the removal of one's covering—is a theme that appears prominently in two Thomas verses; and there are other references to "garments", which depict them as hiding one's true self. ("It is like being draped with unnecessary clothes," notes Bart Ehrman.)

But although there is not a single mention of baptism, in any form, in all of Thomas (in fact, Jesus even speaks against rituals, twice), a lone commentator concludes that the shedding of garments "could refer to a baptism ritual, wherein the participants disrobe."

Another scholar focuses on the garments rather than their removal, and concludes:

> "The garment seems to have some more evocative, definite reference. In a later monastic environment, it could easily have referred to the *habit* worn by monks..."

In another verse, Jesus says that "every female who makes herself male will enter the domain" (having said earlier that this sameness is "so that the male will not be male nor the female be female"); one of the commentators posits that "women philosophers often disguised themselves as men"!

Another scholar, again, has suggested that such "making the two one" sayings may "imply the ideal of sexual continence," having to do with the perception of sameness leading to cessation of attraction to the opposite sex.

Of another verse—where Jesus says, "there is nothing hidden which will not become manifest" (saying not one word about corpses or their resurrection), a scholar interprets this to indicate

> "...the dead body which was made invisible by burial will become visible at the resurrection."

17

And in a verse (of 86 words) in which there is nothing that claims that Jesus "came from above," nor "has come from God," one scholar uses this verse as an indication that "Jesus came from above"; and another scholar, that Jesus "has come from God."

Also, where Jesus says that a person who asks "about the place of life...will become a single one," a writer postulates that (even though the point is that Jesus states "*that* person will live") the meaning

> "...is associated with the notion of androgyny. Some Gnostic groups held that the origin of human sin was the creation of woman as distinct from man, a departure from the sexually non-differentiated first human, Adam. Thus, the ultimate human destiny was to return to a primordial state of androgyny, the state of divine perfection before the fall."

As a final example, Jesus says in verse 39 that the Talmudic religious authorities "have taken the keys of knowledge (gnosis) and hidden them." The analyst has written that this seems to have some association "with the law and its interpretation; one could plausibly argue that it has something to do with [Jewish] dietary laws."

The failure to consider the verses in Thomas outside of the narrow confines of a conventional religious context brings to mind the lines of William Blake: "Both read the Bible day and night. But thou read'st black where I read white."

While there is no historical evidence that Jesus was influenced by nondual teachings (even from so far away as the East), it is not inconceivable that he was. In fact, there is a possibility that at least some of its principles may have been known to him. Let's look at how these teachings may have been present in his time and place.

The writer Holger Kersten provided some research to buttress his points (which otherwise are tenuous) in the Penguin book *Jesus Lived In India*. He attributes "the worldwide spread of Buddhism, even before the pre-Christian era" to the Indian ruler Ashoka, who lived circa 273–232 B.C., and who sent Buddhist missionaries along the Silk Route to as far away as Egypt, Syria, and Greece. The Buddha himself was said to have instructed, "Go, O monks, and travel afar, for the benefit and welfare of many, out of compassion for the world..."

Buddha, like Jesus, had kept on the move, traversing "the entire length of the mid-Ganges basin," says Kersten.

At various times during the history of Buddhism, "the Indies basin, the upper Ganges basin and the Deccan" were invaded by "Hellenic Bactrians of the 2nd Century B.C., and the Scythians and Parthians in the 1st Century B.C. ... The Scythian rulers of the Kushan dynasty themselves encouraged the spread of Buddhism after their own conversion."

Kersten's tracing of cross-fertilization between cultures of the East and Near East, centuries before Jesus' birth, is reflected in the book of Acts (2:9): Parthians (and "residents of Asia") were among those "staying in Jerusalem," even after the crucifixion, this New Testament book says.

Similarly, the Quaker Albert Edmunds, a translator who worked with both Greek and Pali texts, reported on research that was available at the time he wrote *Buddhist and Christian Gospels*, in 1908.

He noted that a German New Testament scholar had initiated such comparisons before him, in 1867, because

> "These parallels [between Buddhist and Christian scriptures] have aroused the interest of New Testament scholars... [since they] belong to a world of [spiritual] thought which the whole East had in common."

Edmunds says that Ashoka (or Asoka) sent Buddhist "missionaries" to five Greek emperors, including Antiochus, Ptolemy and Alexander, between 262–258 B.C.; thus they would have entered Athens, Antioch, and Alexandria. Ptolemy had funded a Greek translation of the Jewish Pentateuch, and reportedly was interested in a similar project concerning Hindu scriptures.

Cross-culturally, Edmunds said that Greek forces inhabited the Punjab, of the Brahmins, around 110 B.C.

In the 2nd Century B.C., there were "Hindu mahouts on the elephants of the Syrian Army."

In the 1st Century B.C., the Roman poet Horace mentions an Indian embassy to the first Roman emperor, Augustus, in 17 B.C.—only a short time before the birth of Jesus.

The Greek geographer Strabo noted, according to Edmunds: "at the time of Christ, the intercourse [East/Near East] was at its height."

And later, Clement of Alexandria, toward the end of the 2nd Century C.E., knew of Hindu "philosophers... who obey the precepts of Buddha."

In any event, it is noteworthy that the author of the Gospel of Matthew did not suppose that his readers would have any difficulty in accepting the arrival, in Judea, of "wise men" (Magi) from the East, from far enough away to need to navigate by the stars (2:1-12) at the time of Jesus' birth.

It is interesting, in this natal tale, that the *first* of those to recognize the true nature of Jesus *were* from the East.

In one of the apocryphal ("hidden") writings, the *Gospel of the Nazarenes*, there is a reputed description of these "foreign travellers" by Joseph: "their appearance is different from our own; their clothing is very rich and their skin quite dark…" However, this may well just be an elaboration on Matthew's birth narrative, which scholars do not find credible.

But that is not to say that there were not Magi in the time of Jesus. Prof. Amy-Jill Levine of Vanderbilt University Divinity School reports:

> "In fact, the Magi in antiquity occasionally carried the reputation of engaging in impolitic action and not doing what the government wanted, so much so that the Roman historian Suetonius tells us that Tiberius, the emperor, banished all Magi from Rome in the year 19 C.E."

The translator Albert Edmunds considered that he had catalogued more than a hundred parallels between Buddhist teachings and the New Testament gospel scriptures they antedated.

In our own day, the well-known scholar of these gospels, Marcus Borg, has produced his own comparisons, in the book *Jesus and Buddha*, and the connections he has deduced are not typical of such scholars in his consideration of Jesus' "role as a 1st Century sage."

He remarks that,

> "...according to the book of Acts, the earliest name for the Jesus movement was 'the Way'. The Gospel of John thus only takes this image one step further in speaking of Jesus as the incarnation of 'the way'. What Jesus and the Buddha said about 'the way' is remarkably similar."

Aside from the fact that Buddha reportedly taught for 45 years after his enlightenment, until his death (given as 483 B.C.), and Jesus from one to (possibly) four years, "Jesus and Buddha were teachers of a world-subverting *wisdom*... an alternative wisdom: they taught a way, or path, of *transformation*...."

> "The similarity is so strong that some scholars have suggested direct contact or 'cultural borrowing' as the explanation. Because the Buddha lived about 500 years earlier than Jesus, the direction of borrowing would have been from Buddha to Jesus....

> "Scholars have pointed out that Buddhist teachers lived in Alexandria, on the Mediterranean coast of Egypt, by the first century.... They also point to the monsoon winds, which by Jesus' day were carrying trading boats from India to Egypt."

Borg details the significant similarities:

> "Jesus and the Buddha had life-transforming experiences of 'the sacred'... the unborn, uncreated, undifferentiated formless source

of all that is—present 'right here' as well as 'more than right here'... the sacred *reality* beyond all personalized *conceptions* of God."

He adds:

"One sees differently after such an experience, and knows something one didn't know before. What one comes to know is the way things really are...."

This "something one didn't *know* before," *spiritually*, is what is known as *gnosis*. Here are just a few of the sayings ascribed to Buddha, collected by Borg, which could fit into the paradigm of the Gospel of Thomas.

That great cloud rains down on all, whether their nature is superior or inferior. The light of the sun and the moon illuminates the whole world, both him who does well and him who does ill; both him who stands high and him who stands low.

*

... these Brahmins teach a path that they do not know... just as a file of blind men go on, clinging to each other, and the first one sees nothing, the middle one sees nothing, and the last one sees nothing—so it is with the talk of these Brahmins.

*

A treasure that... no thief can steal; a treasure which does not pass away.

*

Such talk on the dharma is not given to lay people clothed in white. Such talk on the dharma is given to those who have gone forth.

23

Quotations of the Buddha, similar to the following, have caused some theologians to delve more deeply into Eastern scriptures: "You are my children, I am your father; through me, you have been released from your sufferings... I, myself having attained salvation, am a savior of others...."

A popular American monk, Brother David Steindl-Rast, has written that Thomas Merton "could not have understood the Christian tradition as he did except from the Buddhist perspective."

He goes on to say that on All Saints Day, "in our petitions in the monastery, all the great teachers from the Buddhist and Hindu traditions are being mentioned nowadays, without anybody batting an eyelash."

One other element of the lifeline between the East and the Near East may be present in pre-Christian history.

Alexander the Great (356–323 B.C.), an encyclopedia says, "brought Greek ideas and the Greek way of doing things to all the countries he conquered"; that is, "much of what was then the civilized world"— from Greece to Egypt to Palestine and well into India.

He "reached the rich plains of India in 326 B.C. [and] sailed down the Indus River."

Before he died (after acquiring malaria), he had planned to "combine the best of the East with the West."

The Greek presence in the area of Palestine lasted, according to one source, from 331 B.C. until 146 B.C. when the Romans ruled. Even after the Roman conquest, the Greek language continued to be common in the subjected lands.

The New Testament gospels were evidently originally written in Greek, decades after the death of Jesus. The Coptic text of Thomas, unearthed at Nag Hammadi, appears to have been a translation from an earlier Greek version. Pagels says Thomas addresses a "Greek-speaking audience."

Greek was sometimes spoken in Jesus' Galilee, according to Bart Ehrman (whom we'll introduce soon). Of Jesus specifically, he says: "some historians have surmised that, living in Galilee where Greek was widely known, he may have learned some" (in addition to his native Aramaic).

At Mark 7:26, Jesus is described as having a conversational dialogue with a woman who "was a Greek." It seems unlikely that she would have spoken the Semitic language of Aramaic, so Jesus may have spoken Greek.

The collective scholars of the Jesus Seminar have written concerning Jesus:

> "There is now evidence that suggests he may have been bilingual; Greek was probably his second language, learned from the pagan environment that surrounded him in Galilee, especially in Sepphoris, a hellenistic city located only four miles from his home village. In any case, the written gospels were all composed in Greek, and judging by the poetic shape of much of the language, it seems certain that the Jesus tradition took its formative shape in Greek as well. If Jesus did not speak Greek, very few of his original words have come down to us."

While there's no historical evidence either way, at this point, that Jesus was conversant with Buddhist or Hindu spiritual precepts, there is historical support for its *possibility* through *both* the Greek and the Roman interchange with spiritual emissaries from as far east as India even during Jesus' lifetime.

Pagels has pointed to some noteworthy references:

> "In the early twentieth century, the New Testament scholar Wilhelm Bousset, who traced gnosticism to ancient Babylonian and Persian sources, declared that gnosticism is first of all a pre-Christian movement which had roots in *itself.* It is therefore to be understood...in its own terms, and not as an offshoot or byproduct of the Christian religion.'"

And:

> "In 1934—more than ten years before the Nag Hammadi discoveries—two important new books appeared. Professor Hans Jonas, turning from the question of the historical sources of gnosticism, asked where it originated *existentially.* Jonas suggested that gnosticism emerged in a certain attitude toward existence. He pointed out that the political apathy and cultural stagnation of the Eastern empire, in the first two centuries of this era, coincided with the influx of Oriental religion into Hellenistic culture."

As Paul remarks in 1 Corinthians 1:22, "Greeks look for wisdom."

How unlikely is it that Jesus might have been influenced by teachings that preceded him by centuries? Consider this comparison:

Said to be a contemporary of Jesus, Apollonius of Tyana, an "itinerant sage," is known to have been an exponent of the teachings of Pythagoras, who was born circa 521 B.C. (about 40 years before Buddha).

After receiving an education in the Greek city of Tarsus, Apollonius then traveled to Babylon, an account says, to study with the Magi. Then he went to India to learn first-hand the teachings of the Brahmans. Returning to the coast of northern Syria, Anatolia and Greece, he lead a circle of disciples as a holy man. He also traveled to Rome, Sicily, Spain and visited the "naked sages" of Upper Egypt. Then he lived for the rest of his life in Asia Minor, and died in 96 C.E.*

However, whether or *not* Jesus was influenced by the nondual winds of the East, one needs to consider that there have been the spontaneous awakenings of self-realized sages chronicled in widespread places and times throughout written history—from Buddha, as an example in ancient times, to Ramana Maharshi, as a paragon in modern times.

What later became known as *gnosis* would have been known in Buddha's times as *jnana* (*ya*-na); both mean "knowledge," in the sense of "wisdom," and are evidently related words from the same root.

The meaning of *jnana*, summarized in an encyclopedia, is the "*eradication* of the ignorance that sees the illusory multiplicity of the world as real, by attainment of knowledge of the Self [Absolute]," which is regarded as "a single fundamental reality," by the presence of

---

* Like Jesus, he practiced exorcism and reportedly revived the dead; and, like Jesus, an account of his life didn't appear until well after his death. His followers and those of Jesus knew each other, and debated their leader's merits.

27

which "there is no real distinction between the soul [or self] and God."

As has been said by Ramana Maharshi, "It is due to *illusion*—caused by the ego, the 'I am the body' idea—that the kingdom of God is conceived to be elsewhere."

And the late Jiddu Krishnamurti, a "spiritual philosopher" who reported a spontaneous enlightenment experience,* once made this statement—apparently independently, although it could fit easily into the Gospel of Thomas:

> Under every stone and leaf, that which is eternal exists. But we do not know how to look for it. Our minds and hearts are filled with other things than the understanding of 'what is'.

There is *gnosis* and there are *Gnostics*. *Gnosis* is defined as "spiritual knowledge or insightful wisdom attained by self-illumination." *Gnosticism* is defined as "a dualistic religious system that combines ideas from mythology, philosophy and the abstruse."

As an encyclopedia puts it: "*Gnosis*, as concerned with the Eternal, was already present in earlier Greek interest, but its connection with the later Gnostic *movement* is distant at *best*....Much of early Christianity's *doctrine* was formulated in *reaction* to" Gnosticism's unorthodoxy.

A person who professes to be a member of the Gnostic sect may or may not possess spiritual wisdom attained by self-illumination—just

---

* In correspondence with Annie Besant at the time.

as a member of today's Masonic Order may or may not know how to construct a brick tower. Most likely, *rarely* will there be an exemplar of either the former or of the latter.

Consequently, gnosis may sometimes be present where Gnostics are present, but Gnostics are not always present where gnosis is present.

The religious-studies scholars seem generally incapable of drawing this distinction. They often, in other words, confuse the nondual precepts with the doctrine of Gnosticism—which by definition is a dualistic theology.

This is particularly evident as pertains to the Gospel of Thomas, and it is this misconstruction that needs to be addressed by these academics.

Whatever connection that the composition, known as the Gospel of Thomas, may *presumably* have had to some (unknown) Gnostic denomination, the overall message carried in its 114 logia (or verses) can be interpreted as having its roots in ancient nondual insight.

Overall, these sayings in Thomas cannot be made sense of in a dualistic context, whether they were pondered by Gnosticism's readers or *not*.

Nor, likewise, is its message likely to be comprehended by—dualistic —*Christian* readers. (More about this later.[*])

Gnosti*cism*, as a doctrinal development, has been defined by one scholar thus:

> "Gnosticism is the notion that the world is evil, the result of a rebellious angel (demiurge) attempting to create *something apart*

---

[*] See the section beginning page 139.

from God. The goal (end) of the Gnostic's existence is to escape the created world and return to the state of perfection that existed in the beginning, before the creation of the world."

Bertil Gärtner, of Sweden, pointed out that when *he* employs the word *Gnostic* or *Gnosticism*, it is to denote

"...all those syncretistic [various] streams in the early Church which differed from the main traditions... and which finally led to a split with the Church.

"It is terribly difficult, on these matters, to draw the line... due to our basic inability either to find a common denominator for 'Gnosticism' or to decide the date at which we can really begin to talk about 'Gnosticism.'"

He says of Thomas,

"...the basic point of view of this gospel presupposes ideas totally *different* from those of the New Testament... and the material is, at the same time, *far* from typically Gnostic."

Pagels agrees:

"Many of us are discussing questions like whether it is misleading to classify these texts as Gnostic."

Luke Timothy Johnson, Professor of New Testament and Christian Origins at Emory University, received his Ph.D. at Yale and taught at Yale Divinity School. He was for nine years a Benedictine monk, and is author of several books and a lecturer on a few audio courses. He has remarked: "The term 'Gnosticism' covers such a complex set of religious phenomena that some scholars challenge the very concept..." Aside from Christianity, it is used "for religious tendencies in Judaism and Greco-Roman culture."

And Richard Valantasis, Associate Professor of Early Christian Literature at Saint Louis University, says,

> "...as a religious tendency or phenomenon, gnosticism is suspected to exist in other religious and philosophical writings of the first century BC, and the first centuries CE."

Stephen Patterson, Assistant Professor of New Testament at Eden Theological Seminary, says, "it has often been pointed out that Thomas lacks the characteristics of a full-blown Gnosticism, such as an elaborate mythological framework..."

He says that scholar Steven Davies is:

> "...correct in pointing out that Thomas is not a full-blown gnostic gospel, complete with their typically intricate descriptions of the cosmos, the origin of the world, and other features common to later gnostic tractates. But neither is Thomas simply a book of Jewish wisdom speculation....

> "Rather, what we have in Thomas is a book which stands between the wisdom collection, on the one hand, and the gnostic revelation dialogue in which the redeemer reveals to his followers secret words of knowledge, on the other."

This is important hindsight and self-critique which is taking place among these analysts, because the Gospel of Thomas has been misunderstood from the beginning to be merely an offshoot of early Christian theology.

Valantasis has written:

"The argument in the academy has mostly centered upon this Gospel's fit in relationship to other gospel material, as opposed to what this Gospel *says*...

"The previous work has brought us all to the point that there is some need for a fresh start, a new and vigorous reading of these sayings .... it requires *not* reading the Gospel of Thomas in relationship to the synoptic traditions, and *not* reading it in relationship to the fully developed gnostic systems of the second century."

Bertil Gärtner admits,

"When we are working with texts such as these...we are constantly dealing with words which carry different implications from those which they have in New Testament or Christian theology. This can in fact lead the analyst totally astray."

Bart Ehrman is Professor of Religious Studies at the University of North Carolina at Chapel Hill, and has been Director of Graduate Studies there. He received a Masters of Divinity degree and Ph.D. magna cum laude at Princeton Theological Seminary, and taught at Rutgers for four years.

A New Testament and Early Christianity specialist, he has authored or edited 17 books, and is a popular lecturer at universities. Among his books are *Lost Scriptures: Books That Did Not Make It into the New Testament*, and *The Orthodox Corruption of Scriptures: The Effect of Early Christological Controversies on the Text of the New Testament*. He is often quoted, due to his extensive expertise and objectivity.

Ehrman, who also has taped a number of excellent courses for The Teaching Company, has called Gnosticism an "umbrella term" which has "befuddled modern scholars," who have had "enormous and ongoing disputes" concerning "the overall phenomenon traditionally called Gnosticism"—especially "whether the Gospel of Thomas is Gnostic at all."

He adds, "while it is one thing to summarize the gist of the teachings of one Gnostic group or another, it is another thing to plumb the depths of the [Library] texts themselves," especially their "subtle nuances of highly symbolic language…. Some of them are evidently not even Gnostic…"

Another authority, Richard Smith, mentions that

> "…none of the Nag Hammadi texts use 'gnostic' as a term of self-designation…. With the publication of the Nag Hammadi library, the study of ancient Gnosticism has become increasingly problematic—so likewise its relevance. The frequently-attempted etymological definition (gnostic comes from the Greek word for know) is frustratingly inadequate.
>
> "We do better to avoid generalizations, and to marvel at the variety of the sources."

The highly-respected scholar John Dominic Crossan goes even further: "Was gnosticism… an original ideology or religion that arose independently" of Judaism or Jesus?

He answers:

> "George MacRae highlighted some of the evidence of *pre*-Christian gnosticism… and concluded that 'for a growing number of scholars

—now clearly in the majority—such evidence...enables us to *rule out*...that Gnosticism is to be seen as a heretical *offshoot* from Christianity."

It's not surprising, then, that scholar Michael A. Williams has written a book titled *Rethinking Gnosticism: An Argument for Dismantling a Dubious Category.*

Richard Valantasis says of the Thomas gospel:

> "There seems no longer to be either a consensus about the definition, nor the referent, nor even the chronology and content of gnosticism. The 'gnostic' character of these sayings needs the same sort of re-evaluation as the entire study of gnosticism in early Christianity....
>
> "The scholars who want to identify the theology of Thomas as gnostic, begin with the *assumption* of its gnostic nature and then proceed to justify that characterization through establishing parallels with the theology and mythology of later and fully developed gnosticism."

Translator Marvin Meyer says of the Nag Hammadi texts:

> "Some texts in these codices may be considered Gnostic, while others certainly are *not*. Further, in scholarly discussions, the term Gnostic itself is an embattled term...the words gnōsis (gnosis), gnōstikos, and gnōstikoi (from which the English word Gnostic and Gnostics, respectively, are derived) are ancient Greek words; but the term Gnosticism (with the ending –ism) is a modern word that was coined in the seventeenth century."

Elaine Pagels is another eminent scholar who has reflected on this entire issue. For example, she has noticed:

"Another book discovered at Nag Hammadi, *On the Origin of the World*, says that when the first man and woman recognized their nakedness, 'they saw that they were naked of spiritual understanding (gnosis)'. But then the luminous *epinoia* 'appeared to them shining with light, and *awakened their consciousness*.'"

She defines *gnostic* as a person who claims to know about "ultimate reality."

"But gnosis is not primarily *rational* knowledge. The Greek language distinguishes between scientific or reflective knowledge ('He knows mathematics') and knowing through observation or *experience* ('He knows me'), which is *gnosis*. As the gnostics use the term, we could translate it as 'insight', for *gnosis* involves an intuitive process of knowing *oneself*."

She then quotes from an excellent summary concerning gnosis.

"Yet to know oneself, at the deepest level, is simultaneously to know God; this is the secret of gnosis. Another gnostic teacher, Monoimus, says:

'Abandon the search for "God" and the "creation", and other matters of a similar sort. Look for him by taking your self as the starting point. Learn who it is within you who makes everything his own and says, my God, my mind, my thought, my soul, my body.... Learn the sources of sorrow, joy, love, hate.... If you carefully investigate these matters you will find him *in yourself*.'"

Pagels points out some meaningful distinctions:

"Orthodox Jews and Christians insist that a chasm separates humanity from its creator: God is wholly 'other'. But some of the gnostics who wrote *these* gospels contradict this: self-knowledge is knowledge of God; the self and the divine are identical.

"Second, the living Jesus of these texts speaks of illusion and enlightenment, not of sin and repentance like the Jesus of the New Testament. Instead of 'coming to save us from sin', he comes as a guide who opens access to spiritual understanding. But when the disciple attains enlightenment, Jesus no longer serves as his spiritual master: the two have become equal—even identical." *

And she arrives at the critical question:

"Does not such teaching—the identity of the divine-and-human; the concern with illusion and enlightenment; the founder who is presented not as Lord, but as spiritual guide—sound more Eastern than Western? Some scholars have suggested that if the names were changed, the 'living Buddha' appropriately could say what the Gospel of Thomas attributes to the living Jesus. Could Hindu or Buddhist tradition have influenced gnosticism?"

She adds:

"The British scholar of Buddhism, Edward Conze, suggests that it had. He points out that Buddhists were in contact with the Thomas Christians (that is, Christians who knew and used such writings as the Gospel of Thomas) in South India. Trade routes between the Greco-Roman world and the Far East were opening up at the time when gnosticism flourished (A.D. 80–200); *for generations*, Buddhist missionaries had been proselytizing in Alexandria. We note that Hippolytus, who was a Greek-speaking Christian in Rome

---

* Or "single", as the verses put it.

(c. 225), knows of the Indian Brahmins—and includes their tradition among the sources of heresy."

Hippolytus commented: "There is…among the Indians a heresy of those who philosophize among the Brahmins," who speak of "knowledge (gnosis) through which the secret mysteries of nature are perceived by the wise."

Pagels concludes:

"Could the title of *The Gospel of Thomas*—named for the disciple who, tradition tells us, went to India—suggest the influence of Indian tradition?"

Dr. Marvin Meyer, Professor of Bible and Christian Studies at Chapman University, is one of the foremost authorities on Gnosticism; the Nag Hammadi Library (having edited the first edition of the English translation); and so-called apocryphal, or non-canonical, texts.

He has studied the

"…early form of spirituality that emphasizes gnōsis, or 'knowledge'—mystical knowledge; knowledge of God and *the essential oneness of the self with God.* This spirituality is commonly described as 'gnostic,' but there was a debate in the ancient world over the use of the term, and that debate continues to the present day among scholars. Such a direct approach to God as is to be found in gnostic spirituality requires no intermediary—after all, God is the spirit and light within—and the evidence from the early Church, and the heresiologists (heresy hunters) within the Church, indicates that the priests and bishops were not pleased with these free-thinking gnostics."

37

In gnostic texts,

> "Jesus is primarily a teacher and revealer of wisdom and knowledge, not a savior who dies for the sins of the world. For gnostics, the fundamental problem in human life is not sin, but ignorance; and the best way to address this problem is not through faith but through knowledge."

And, Meyer says,

> "If scholars are correct in their understanding of the development of gnostic traditions, the roots of these ideas may go back to the first century, or even before, within Jewish philosophical and gnostic circles that were open to Greco-Roman ideas..."

Meyer gives this overall assessment of the gnostics' view:

> "The knowledge claimed by these people is not worldly knowledge but mystical knowledge, knowledge of God-and-self, and the 'relationship' between God and self... the most profound mystery of the universe is that within some human beings is the spirit of the divine. Although we live in a flawed world that too often is the domain of darkness and death, we can transcend darkness and embrace life...

> "If Jesus is the son of the divine, so also are all of *us* children of the divine. All we need to do is to live out of that knowledge of the divine, and we shall be enlightened...

> "If people come to know their true divine selves, they will be able to escape the clutches of the powers of this world and realize the peace of enlightenment."

And:

"Gnostics texts employ various figures of speech to depict the sorry fate of the entrapped spirit: it is asleep, drunk, sick, ignorant, and in darkness. In order to be liberated, then, the spirit needs to be awakened and brought to sobriety, wholeness, knowledge, and enlightenment."

Marcus Borg, also, comments that Jesus

"...used the forms of 'wisdom' to subvert conventional ways of seeing. His proverbs and parables often reversed ordinary perception, functioning to jolt his hearers out of their present *world*, their present way of seeing reality...

"Finally, however, his teaching involved more than a subverting of conventional wisdom. He affirmed another vision and another way. He taught an alternative way of being and an alternative consciousness, shaped by the relationship to Spirit and not primarily by the dominant consciousness of culture. He was thus not only a subversive sage but a transformative sage...the heart of his teaching: the path of transformation is a dying to the self and to the world."

A *gnostic*, then, primarily wants to "know" divinity, not merely *believe* that there *is* divinity—*experiencing* divinity just as Jesus had claimed to so do.

As Ramana Maharshi has stated:

The absolute Being is what it is. It is the Self. It is God. Knowing the Self, God is known. In fact, God is none other than the Self.

In other words, the "knowing" is to recognize that God can't be *known* as something apart from the person who would know.

As Anglican Bishop N. T. Wright has concluded, "The core Christian teaching is wrong, if the gnostics are right."

Since gnosis is the wisdom that the spiritual, or divine, cannot be experienced as a reality apart from oneself, this is why the ancient scriptures describe this transformative insight, or epiphany, as "non-dual realization."

◎

Let us look more closely at such teachings, and their relevance to the Gospel of Thomas.

Philosopher of Religion Don Cupitt has given a suitable summary of what he has termed "mystical theology" (as it would apply to Meister Eckhart's discourse):

> "[As] the First Principle, or self-founding foundation of all things, 'God' is absolutely one and simple, as well as being infinite.
>
> "God has no body, *parts*, or *passions*...no structure. There is in God no *differentia*, no *contrast*, nothing that one might be able to single out or get hold of.
>
> "Nor can one draw any '*nearer*' to God, because God is *omnipresent* in whole reality, everywhere.... We always already *coincide*, with a God who is always unknowable.... And the state of 'resting in God' may *equally* well be described as a state of absolute knowledge...the way to it is by dismantling, dissolving away, the 'realistic' doctrines of both God *and* the self...
>
> "Admittedly, the *spiritual* message is a deadly heresy.... The dissolution of God, and our attainment of perfect union with God, are one and the *same* thing."

Bart Ehrman has reflected much of this basic description of the nondual perspective, in some of his comments on what "salvation" alludes to in the logia of Thomas.

He points out, first of all, that "ancient [i.e., pagan: neither Jewish nor Christian] religions had no *beliefs* to affirm, theologies to embrace or creeds to recite."

Specifically, regarding the Gnostic message,

> "The key to salvation brought by Jesus is having the proper knowledge, gnosis—knowledge of your *true* identity...

> "This salvation comes from knowing the sayings of Jesus and interpreting them correctly. On the other hand, those who do not accept the true knowledge will face death...

> "Salvation, then, comes by acquiring the true knowledge that can bring... a liberation that is sometimes portrayed as *awakening* from a dream, or becoming sober after being drunk...

> "Salvation here does not come by the 'death and resurrection' of Jesus, but by the knowledge that he imparts to those who can understand...

> "Salvation, then, comes with being *one*—or reunified—with the divine entity from which you have been divided. As Thomas puts it, whoever will be saved must become a solitary—or a single— united one." *

Concluding Ehrman's interpretation: "It is by knowing yourselves that you achieve knowledge of salvation. *You* are a divine being..."

---

* As Pagels has pointed out, the terms *monk* and *monastic* come from a Greek word "meaning 'solitary' or 'single one,' which the Gospel of Thomas frequently uses to describe the gnostic."

In Psalms (8:22-23), the voice of Wisdom says:

> *The Lord brought me forth as the first of his works, before his deeds of old; I was appointed from eternity, from the beginning before the world began.*

Spiritual Wisdom and *Divine Light* are often spoken of interchangeably, in the ancient scriptures. In Thomas, Jesus says,

> *"It is I who am the light"* (logion 77),

and to followers:

> *"If they say to you, 'Where did you come from?', say to them, 'We came from the light....'"* (logion 50).

In the Gospel of John (7:14-16), Jesus' listeners are "amazed" when he teaches in the Jerusalem temple courts, and ask:

> *How did this man get such learning without having studied?*

> *Jesus answered, 'My teaching is not my own. It comes from him who sent me.'*

And at Mark 13:11, Jesus tells his disciples, "it is not *you* speaking, but the Holy Spirit."

Pagels notes in various apocryphal writings the similarities, in emphasis, to the concerns of nondual enlightenment.

> "*Zostrianos*, the longest text in the Nag Hammadi library, tells how one spiritual master attained enlightenment, implicitly setting out a program for others to follow."

And:

"In the book of *Thomas the Contender*, another ancient book belonging to Syrian Thomas tradition discovered at Nag Hammadi, 'the living Jesus' addresses Thomas (and, by implication, the reader) as follows: *'Since you are my twin and my true companion, examine yourself, and learn who you are.... Since you will be called my [twin],... although you do not understand it yet... you will be called "the one who knows himself." For whoever has not known himself, knows nothing; but whoever has known himself has simultaneously come to know the depth of all things.'"*

"...the author of the *Secret Book* [of James] invokes a cluster of words related to the Greek verb *noein*, which means 'perceive,' 'think,' or 'be aware.' The *Secret Book* explains that, although God is essentially incomprehensible, the powers that *reveal* God to humankind include *pronoia* (anticipatory awareness), *ennoia* (internal reflection), and *prognosis* (foreknowledge or intuition)..."

Also, from the *Secret Book of John*, Jesus says:

So it is possible for you, too, to receive for yourselves heaven's domain: unless you receive it through knowledge, you will not be able to discover it.

And:

Don't be arrogant about the light that enlightens.

In *Jesu Christi Sophia*, Jesus says:

*He who has ears to hear with, let him hear about the eternal things. I will speak with those who are awake.**

---

* The word *Buddha*, incidentally, means "awakened". The enlightened Buddha declared of himself, "I am awake."

Jesus says to Thomas, in another Library tractate which is later than the Gospel of Thomas:

> *For he who has not known himself has known nothing, but* he who has *known himself has at the same time already achieved* knowledge about the depth of the all. *So, then, you, my brother Thomas, have beheld what is obscure to men, that is, what they ignorantly stumble against.*

And from another tractate, *Allogenes*, the description of the Absolute, or One (spoken of here as "he"), would be recognized by anyone familiar with the nondual teachings:[*]

> *[He exists] as an Invisible One who is incomprehensible to them all. He contains them all within (himself), for (they) all exist because of (him). He is perfect, and he is (greater) than perfect, and he is blessed. (He is) always (One) and (he) exists (in) them all, being ineffable, unnameable, (being One) who exists through (them all)—he whom, (should) one discern (him, one would not desire) anything that (exists) before him among those (that possess) existence; for (he is) the (source from which they were all emitted. He is prior to perfection. He was prior to every) divinity, (and) he is prior (to) every blessedness since he provides for every power. And he (is) a nonsubstantial substance…*

> *(It is not impossible for them) to receive a (revelation of) these things if (they) come together. Since it is impossible for the (individuals) to comprehend the Universal One (situated in the) place that is higher than perfect, they apprehend by means of a First (Thought)—(it is) not as Being (alone), (but) it is along with the latency of Existence that he confers Being. He (provides) everything for (himself) since it is he who shall come to be when he (recognizes himself). And he is (One) who subsists as a (cause) and source (of Being) and (an) immaterial (material and an) innumerable (number and a formless) form and a (shapeless) shape…*

---

[*] Parenthetical extrapolations by the translator here and elsewhere.

The unmistakable description of the One in this tractate, *Trimorphic Protennoia*, is as clear as in the Bhagavad Gita:

I dwell in those who came to be. I move in everyone and I delve into them all. I walk uprightly, and those who sleep I (awaken). And I am the sight of those who dwell in sleep. I am the Invisible One within the All. It is I who counsel those who are hidden, since I know the All that exists in it. I am numberless beyond everyone. I am immeasurable, ineffable, yet whenever I (wish, I shall) reveal myself of my own accord. I (am the head of) the All. I exist before the (All, and) I am the All, since I (exist in) everyone ... "

And I hid myself in everyone and revealed (myself) within them, and every mind seeking me longed for me, for it is I who gave shape to the All when it had no form.

Marvin Meyer offers his own translation of this excerpt from the *Book of Thomas* (probably a later composition than the *Gospel* of Thomas). The disciple Thomas says to Jesus, at one point:

You are our light, and you bring enlightenment, Lord.

The Savior answered and said, "If what can be seen is obscure to you, how can you comprehend what cannot be seen?"

Thomas answered, "You have convinced us, Lord. We have come to this realization, and now it is clear; this is as it is, and your word is sufficient for us. But these sayings that you utter are laughable and ridiculous to the world, for they are misunderstood."

Similarly, Meyer's translation of an excerpt from the *Secret Book of John* (or *Apocryphon of John*), from the Library:

When I asked if I might understand this, he said to me, "The One is a sovereign that has nothing over it. It is God and Father of all, the Invisible One that is over all, that is imperishable, that is pure light no eye can see.

"It is the invisible Spirit. One should not think of it as a god, or like a god. For it is greater than a god, because it has nothing over it and no lord above it. It does not exist within anything that is inferior to it, since everything exists only within it. It is eternal, since it does not need anything. For it is absolutely complete: it has never lacked anything in order to be complete."

The *Secret Book of John* proceeds with a long descriptive passage pertaining to the infinite and incomparable nature of the One, using terms that have perennially been significant in the nondual scriptures, such as:

It is illimitable… unobservable… eternal… unnameable… holy… perfect in its imperishability.

Not that it is part of perfection… It is neither corporeal nor incorporeal…. It is not one among many things that are in existence; it is much greater.

The point of this kind of "empty" description, as Bertil Gärtner said, "is to demonstrate that human expressions are useless when it comes to dressing the deepest gnosis in words. Christ, in his conversation with John, finally gives up his attempt to *explain* the secrets which contain his knowledge…" To know it, one must know that one *is* it; as Jesus says, "For none of us came to know how it is with the Unfathomable, except the one who has lived *in* it."

◎

46

At this point, it is instructive to consider the substance of the nondual teachings of Ramana Maharshi.

Ramana was highly regarded by such figures as Carl Jung, Mahatma Gandhi, and the Dalai Lama, who acknowledged, "Ramana Maharshi's spiritual wisdom is guiding millions of people." Consider Ramana's words in the context of the Gospel of Thomas:

> *Among the many thousand names of God, no name suits God …*
>
> *God is within you…. Because you have given precedence to worldly things, God appears to have receded to the background. If you give up all else and seek him alone, he alone will remain …*
>
> *God, who seems to be non-existent, alone truly exists; whereas the individual, who seems to be existing, is ever non-existent.*
>
> *Sages say that the state in which one thus knows one's own non-existence alone is the glorious supreme knowledge.*

And:

> *You now take it that you are an individual; that there is the universe; and that God is beyond the cosmos. So there is the idea of separateness. This idea must go. For God is not separate from you or the cosmos…he is the source of all, their abiding place and their end. All proceed from him, have their stay in him, and finally resolve into him. Therefore he is not separate.*

Bertil Gärtner comments:

> "As Jesus in Logion 77 says, *I am the All,* so in the *Acts of Peter* 39 (The Vercelli Acts), Peter says about Jesus Christ *Thou art the All and the All is in thee…* Once more we can see how Gnostic or gnosticising texts illustrate and clarify the meaning of expressions in the Gospel of Thomas."

47

And he adds:

> "The *Gospel of Philip*, from Nag-Hammadi, expresses the same idea:
> 'The Father was in the Son, and the Son *in* the Father. *This* is the
> Kingdom of Heaven.'"

According to Pagels:

> "The *Gospel of John*...is a remarkable book that many gnostic
> Christians claimed for themselves and used as a primary source for
> *gnostic* teaching."

Here are just a sampling of statements that can be found in the New
Testament's *Gospel of John*:

We have seen his glory, the glory of the One and Only... (1:14).

*[Jesus says]... Father, just as you are in me and I am in you. May they
[others] also be in us...* (17:20-21).

... so they may be one as we are one. (17:11; repeated at 22)

I in them and you in me. May they be brought to complete unity. (17:23)

Father, though the world does not know you, I know you. (17:25)

I and the Father are one, [upon which "the Jews picked up stones to
stone him"]. (10:30-31)

The fact that even occasional use of words in the Gospel of Thomas
like "father" or "heaven" or "God" could actually have meanings *other*
than the "Trinity" and "Paradise" and "Jehovah" is not entirely lost on
scholars. Here Gärtner speaks of euphemisms for God, such as Spirit:

"These names are valid in the eyes of men, but what this *being* is in itself is *incomprehensible*. The basic idea behind these forms of expression is that 'Father,' 'Son' and other names are merely descriptions of one and the same ineffable Divine Being. I consider it important that we bear this in mind when we encounter some obscurity in the relationship between the Father and Jesus in the *Gospel of Thomas,* expressed partly in the ascription of the term 'the living' to both."

Gärtner quotes from *Jesu Christi Sophia*:

"He (God) is indeed immortal and eternal; he is an Eternal One who was not born. For he who is born shall (also) perish. He who is not born has indeed no beginning. For he who has a beginning (also) has an end. 'Being born' is no part of the nature of the Highest, since birth implies a limitation."

And he says:

"...Jesus and the Father are interpreted as being a unity. According to this view, everything which is said of the Father may be said of the Son, since they are in their heavenly nature identical."

Thus, in the *Gospel of John*, Jesus said to his disciple Thomas: *I am the way, the truth and the life; no one comes to the Father but by me.*

As Ehrman phrases Jesus' point in the Gospel of Thomas: *"Restore* all things *to their* original *unity, where there are no* parts *but only a whole; no above and below, no outside and inside, no male or female."* And no Son apart from the Father.

◎

It is interesting that, despite the unenlightened perspective which most scholars have brought to their analysis, some of Thomas' verses are so transparent that their nondual import can't be avoided.

For example, Gärtner says of Jesus' instruction to "the enlightened man," in logion 106 ("When you make the two into one, you shall be the children of man"):

> "We have already observed the important role played by the concept of 'unity' in the theological thought-world of *The Gospel of Thomas*, as expressive of the state of salvation. Thus to 'make the two into one' implies to bring division to an end and to unite the individual soul-spark with the 'heavenly' world, by means of saving knowledge."

And:

> "In Logion 72, Jesus' denial that he is a 'divider' is to be understood on the basis of the important position of *division* within the Gnostic world of ideas. Jesus' task is in fact that of bringing division to an end. It is as unthinkable that he could do the work of dividing, according to Logion 72, as that he should rebuild the 'house' that he tears down in Logion 71."

There are, true, some occasions on which an insightful approach to this material has been suggested, as when Ehrman states "...there are some assumptions about a particular text that can make better sense of it than others. And it is never simply a case of 'letting the text speak for itself'..." He has recommended:

> "Read through the *Gospel of Thomas* and see if it is possible to interpret some of the non-New Testament sayings without

appealing to [Gnosticism]. What kind of interpretation would you come up with?"

Lastly, even if we treat these sayings as *not* originating with Jesus—as being as anonymous as were the ancient sutras—they can be identified as a general body of nondual teachings, as anyone thoroughly familiar with such established material will recognize.

Pagels has said, with an open mind:

"Since parallel traditions may emerge in different cultures at different times, such ideas could have developed in both places independently. What we call Eastern and Western religions, and tend to regard as separate streams, were not clearly differentiated 2,000 years ago. Research on the Nag Hammadi texts is only beginning: we look forward to the work of scholars who can study these traditions comparatively to discover whether they can, in fact, be traced to Indian sources."

To better comprehend and interpret the Gospel of Thomas, we need to understand a number of developments that have transfigured the man—the teacher portrayed in this Gospel—into the symbolic image that has been characterized in the New Testament, and which consequently has left readers unsatisfied and puzzled by this distorted creation for close to two thousand years.

There have been more books written about Jesus than any other figure in human history. As Johnson has said, "By any standard, Jesus is one of history's most fascinating, compelling, and *illusive* figures." He ponders, "Why does Jesus remain such a compelling figure even for those who consider themselves non-Christian or even non-religious?"

Or as Ehrman has stated, "Jesus of Nazareth is almost certainly the most important figure in the history of Western civilization, a man whose impact on the *course* of history is completely unparalleled."

And yet, according to Ehrman:

> "From the first century A.D., we have hundreds of documents written by pagan authors for all kinds of reasons, as well as numerous public inscriptions and a considerable archive of private letters.
>
> In none of this extensive literary record is Jesus ever mentioned at all. As enormous an impact as Jesus has made on Western culture over the past 2,000 years, in his own day his impact appears to have been practically nil."

Jesus is not mentioned by any Roman authority of the 1st Century, and even as late as the 4th Century was "completely unknown to major political and intellectual leaders" of that time, Ehrman says.

It is noteworthy that the Gospel of John states (7:5) that, during his life of ministry, "even his own brothers did not believe in him."

And Jesus even says of himself (at Matthew 11:19) that he's been described as "a glutton and a drunkard."

Despite such ignoble aspects, here was a man whose wisdom was regarded as revelatory, to the extent that it was recorded by others and circulated as spiritually instructional.

Patterson comments:

> "While we will never be able to say with certainty that Jesus in fact uttered this or that particular wisdom saying, the fact that the

earliest Christian voice we hear [Mark] recollects a Jesus who made ample use of common wisdom warrants serious consideration of the hypothesis that Jesus was a wisdom teacher, and that the early Jesus movement thought of itself as a kind of wisdom school."

The character of this wisdom was that it empowered the listener to realize spiritual truth for *oneself*. As Patterson says, in agreement with Harvard University's Helmut Koester:

"In Thomas, the disclosure of knowledge is always *self*-disclosure. Koester writes:

'Throughout the tradition of these sayings, their truth does not depend upon the authority of Jesus. Whether the wisdom saying envisages man's *being* in general, or whether it discloses man's spiritual nature and origin, its truth is vindicated whenever he finds this truth *in himself*.'"

In fact, it was Jesus' insistence not to depend on others to interpret God for oneself which cast his ministry as essentially a revolt against religious authority.

Jesus (as have other sages) claimed that all that is "godly" or "heavenly" is already in your domain, that the divine "kingdom" is *within* you—blatantly contradicting the conventional religious dogma of his time.

Reportedly persecuted by religious authorities, his parables veiled his spiritual teachings; there are indications that he spoke more openly with a select few. While the later Church purports to have preserved his public pronouncements, his private disclosures—which *might* have been recorded—have remained a mystery.

That Jesus might have reserved his deepest spiritual knowledge for those seekers who were most sincere—and to have transmitted it directly in private—is not surprising. The Vedic teachings were disseminated orally for centuries before their availability in writing, and are believed to have originally been reserved only for the initiate.

Unlike the New Testament gospels, the Gospel of Thomas designates itself a "secret" text. And scholars have been drawn to it because it portends, as Pagels has put it, "other dimensions of meaning," with sayings "as cryptic and compelling as Zen koans."

Jesus was not to *lightly* proclaim deep wisdom that he had risked his life to profess, as Pagels points out:

> "He demanded that those who followed him must give up everything—family, home, children, ordinary work, wealth—to join him. And he himself, as prototype, was a homeless man who rejected his own family, avoided marriage and family life, a mysterious wanderer who insisted on truth at all costs, even the cost of his own life. Mark relates that Jesus concealed his teaching from the masses, and entrusted it only to the few he considered worthy to receive it."

And:

> "Gnostic teachers usually reserved their secret instruction, sharing it only verbally, to ensure each candidate's suitability to receive it. Such instruction required each teacher to take responsibility for highly select, individualized attention to each candidate."

Bertil Gärtner:

> "In the *Gospel of Mary*, Peter requests (on behalf of the disciples) to be told what were the depths of knowledge entrusted to her by

Jesus. She answers, 'I shall tell you what is hidden,' after which follows a description of various central points in the revelation."

"In the *Apocryphon of John*, the gnosis passed on to John by Jesus is characterised as the *mysterion*, which may only be spread in secret. 'But I am telling you (John) this in order that you may write it down and pass it on in secret to your kindred spirits. For this mystery belongs to that family which does not waver.' The mystery is the hidden knowledge of the heavenly secrets, the saving gnosis which is linked in particular with the true nature of the Saviour and with man's share in the light-world."

And:

"Thus it is also common in Gnostic circles to find warnings being issued against sharing gnosis with the unworthy. In the *Apocryphon of John*, Jesus warns against just such a practice with these words: 'Cursed is everyone who communicates it for the sake of a gift, or for the sake of food, or for the sake of drink, or for the sake of clothes, or for the sake of anything similar.'"

Further:

"Man must not allow the material—or for that matter anything belonging to this world—to encroach upon the heavenly. Those who are worthy to receive Jesus' secret doctrine are precisely those who have neither given themselves over to the world nor allowed worldly things to corrupt them."

Also:

"Another document with a close theological affinity to the Gospel of Thomas is the *Acts of Thomas*; in the Greek version of this collection of traditions, are used… a word which is very closely connected to the expression for *revelation*, also said to be hidden. It is a secret mystery. Of Jesus it is said, 'Thou art he that *revealeth* secret mysteries and discloseth words that are secret.' And 'Thou (Jesus) art the heavenly word of the Father: thou art the hidden light of the understanding.'

"The apostle is thus the one who is specially trusted, the one who is 'initiate in the hidden word of Christ, who receivest his secret oracles.' The secret is here also primarily a technical term used to describe the mysteries, and all that belongs to *gnosis*."

Gärtner quotes the venerable scholar Henri-Charles Puech, regarding the purview of *Thomas*:

"It is esoteric—or is considered to be so—and contains secret utterances hidden from the profane, but the understanding of which ensures eternal life for the one who is able to apprehend it."

Among the Library tractates, the *Secret Book of James* also indicates the propensity for secrecy, in the words of its author, as translated by Marvin Meyer:

Since you have asked me to send you a secret book, revealed to me and Peter by the Lord, I could not turn you down or refuse you. So I have written it in Hebrew, and sent it to you and only you. But, considering that you are a minister for the salvation of the saints, try to be careful not to communicate this book to many people, for the Savior did not even want to communicate it to all of us, his twelve disciples.

And elsewhere in that text, it is specified that:

... the twelve disciples were all sitting together and recalling what the Savior had said to each one of them, either secretly or openly, and putting it into books, and I was writing what is in my book.

Also, the *Book* of Thomas (again, thought to be a later composition than the Gospel of Thomas) announces itself thus, according to Marvin Meyer:

> *The secret sayings that the Savior spoke to Judas Thomas and that I, Matthew, recorded as I was walking and listening to them speak with each other.*

> *The Savior said, "Brother Thomas, while you still have time in the world, listen to me and I shall explain what you have been reflecting upon in your mind."*

Not only is it possible that the Gospel of Thomas discloses Jesus' fundamental perspective was that of nonduality, there is evident reason to believe that its pronouncements were recorded e*arlier* than the more elaborated New Testament gospels.

For scholars, a sign that the material of one tradition (such as that of the "Thomas school") is a predecessor to that of other traditions (such as that of the New Testament gospels) is that the material of the earlier stream will be more succinct and direct. The more elaborately a scripture is embroidered, the more likely it is weighted with interpolations.

New Testament experts have noticed that a verse in the Bible will frequently begin with the first sentence or two of Thomas' phrasing and may then run on for several unbroken paragraphs of Christian doctrine.

As Ehrman has stated:

"[a] rule of thumb that historians follow; accounts of Jesus that are clearly imbued with a highly-developed theology are less likely to be historically accurate.... Then there is at least a theoretical possibility that these saying and deeds were made up precisely in order to advance the views that some Christians held dear."

And, Norman Perrin:

"The synoptic tradition, as we have it, is the culmination of a long and complex process of transmission according to the needs, interests, and emphases of the Church. It follows, therefore, that only the earliest form of any saying known to us, and a form *not* reflecting these needs, interests or emphases, has a claim to authority."

◎

While for scholars it is treacherous ground to base analysis on assumptions, one *presumption* that has been rendered rather dubious is the theory that the New Testament gospels had been written prior to the Thomas sayings collection.

The conjecture, thus, is that the Thomas logia were "borrowed" from the province established by Mark, Matthew, Luke, John and even Paul, as well as the book of Acts. Evidence seems to indicate, however, that Thomas was in circulation prior, and may therefore have been known to the New Testament authors as a *source*.

◎

Another clue has been that when the New Testament writers used one another as their source ("...*all* critical scholars agree that one of the Gospels was written first, and the others used it as a literary source for *their* versions."—Johnson), they have tended to place the borrowed material in the same order. However, while Thomas contains some verses that are similar to the New Testament, they do not appear in an order that is similar to those in the Bible.

Therefore, it is generally agreed among most authorities today that Thomas is an "independent" stream, meaning that it was not simply based on the canonical accounts; indeed, there is material in Thomas that has no parallel in the New Testament compositions.

As Ehrman has commented: "Because there are so few verbal parallels, it does not appear that Thomas used the New Testament gospels as one of its sources."

Patterson stated:

> "…one finds little to suggest that the author who compiled the sayings collection known as the Gospel of Thomas was even *aware* of the synoptic texts."

And Crossan cites John Sieber:

> "…he concluded 'that there is very little redactional evidence, if any, for holding that our Synoptic Gospels were the sources of Thomas' (synoptic) sayings. In the great majority of sayings, there is no such evidence at all."

Crossan states:

> "It now appears that a majority of scholars who have seriously investigated the matter have been won over to the side of Thomas' independence of the canonical Gospels, though these scholars hold a variety of views about the actual history of the composition of the Gospel of Thomas."

Gärtner recalls the position of the established scholar Gilles Quispel, who wrote:

"The importance of the Gospel of Thomas lies in the fact that it contains an independent and very *old* gospel tradition. When I say independent, I mean that some sayings of the Gospel of Thomas were not taken from our canonical Gospels, Matthew, Mark, Luke and John, but were borrowed from another source."

Says Gärtner, "This ancient source, according to Quispel, goes back to an Aramaic tradition..." Thus, Thomas:

"should contain a good deal of material of the same historical value as the synoptics. They (these new sayings of Jesus) may have been transmitted in a Palestinian milieu quite *isolated* from the rest of Christendom, and *not* influenced by the trends of Pauline theology. And we must not exclude the possibility that these people may sometimes have preserved the words of Jesus in a form more *primitive than that found in the canonical Gospels.*"

Gärtner says that Quispel considered that this Aramaic tradition,

"may be traced back to the descendents of the primitive community of Jerusalem, who lived on in the Near East almost completely isolated from the Gentile *Christian* developments."

Noting verse 12 in Thomas (where Jesus seems to be suggesting James as his successor), Gärtner comments:

"Here it is James the brother of the Lord who is represented as the central figure among the faithful after the departure of Jesus... —to some extent in opposition to Peter and John, whom the New Testament describes as the leaders."

That the Thomas sayings may be a collection that is earlier than other accounts, and more authentic, has been remarked upon by other analysts.

Johnson:

> "As a possible source for reconstructing the historical Jesus, strong claims have been made for [Thomas]. Some scholars argue that it contains sayings earlier in *form* than in the canonical gospels."

For example, Meyer:

> "Sayings in the Gospel of Thomas also seem to be transmitted in a form that is earlier than what we have in the canonical gospels. Such may be noted, for instance, in parables… The textual evidence for an early date for the Gospel of Thomas thus may rival that of any of the New Testament gospels.
>
> "They may even provide us with earlier versions than the ones in the New Testament."

And:

> "…quite a few may reflect actual sayings of Jesus of Nazareth. There is no good reason to suppose that authentic sayings of Jesus are to be found only in the New Testament."

Patterson remarks on Thomas' sayings:

> "…many must have a history that extends back into the earliest phase of the Jesus movement. Thus, it is possible that from Thomas we can learn something of the preaching of Jesus himself."

Even the Encyclopedia Britannica has commented:

> "...[gnosticism] stressed the redemptive power of esoteric knowledge acquired by divine revelation. For Thomas, salvation consists of self-knowledge... It is, of course, possible or even *likely* that individual sayings in Thomas, or other apocryphal gospels, *originated* with Jesus..."

Ehrman reports that most scholars think that Thomas' author:

> "had heard the sayings of Jesus as they had been transmitted orally, by word of mouth... many of which may represent things Jesus actually taught...

> "Strikingly, some of these sayings are briefer, pithier forms than their New Testament counterparts. Could they be more *authentic* forms of the sayings?"

Also:

> "If Thomas did not use the gospels of the New Testament, is it possible *it* was written earlier than they were? Some sayings found in Thomas may have been spoken by Jesus himself—and thus were around *before* the New Testament Gospels."

Of the *New Testament* accounts, Ehrman says:

> "They were not written by eyewitnesses near the time of the events they describe, but by authors who lived later, in different parts of the world; who were biased toward their subject; who are not completely consistent with one another; and who inherited their stories from an oral tradition which had undergone serious alteration...

"In general terms, we are best served to give particular weight to the *earliest* sources, and to sources that appear to provide a portrayal of Jesus that is not overly-developed theologically; moreover, the particular biases and emphases of all our sources must be considered."

Helmut Koester, a highly regarded professor who has been editor of *Harvard Theological Review*, has said that:

"...many of the [Thomas] sayings (like the oldest sayings of the canonical gospels) were certainly first circulated in Aramaic, the language of Jesus.

"If one considers the form and wording of the individual sayings in comparison with the form in which they are preserved in the New Testament, The Gospel of Thomas almost always appears to have preserved a more original form of the traditional saying... More original and shorter forms are especially evident in the parables of Thomas."

Further:

"The Gospel of Thomas, in its oldest form, stressed the finding of wisdom—of the kingdom of the father—in the knowledge (gnosis) of oneself, *guided* by the *sayings* of Jesus...which speak of the knowledge of one's divine origin—which [knowledge] even Adam did not share, although 'he came into being from a great power.'"

"Salvation is obtained by stripping off everything ["garment"] that is of this world.... Even women can attain this goal, if they achieve the 'maleness' of the solitary existence."

Koester has concluded, "it is not possible to ascribe the work to any particular *gnostic* school or sect."

Scholar James H. Charlesworth sums it up by saying:

> "...it is now becoming well recognized that it is improper to discard the Gospel of Thomas as late [in composition], derivative [from the New Testament], and gnostic [in terms of Gnosticism]."

In 1985, thirty religious-studies scholars gathered in the U.S. under the name of the Jesus Seminar, to pool their individual specialties concerning what can credibly be known about Jesus, his words and his deeds. In gatherings thereafter, some two hundred academic specialists were attracted because, as a spokesperson has said, "The level of public knowledge of the Bible borders on the illiterate."

As Johnson has described the mission:

> "The Jesus Seminar, founded in 1985 by Robert Funk, is only the most visible component in this new quest to find a Jesus who is unencumbered by Christian doctrine."

Many important and worthwhile treatises have been written for the public and published by the Seminar scholars (some of whom are informational sources in this book), and the Gospel of Thomas has been included in their research.

According to the Jesus Seminar, the Gospel of Thomas "may have originated as early as 50–60 C.E...... It is a wisdom gospel made up of the teachings of a sage...."

> "He reminds his followers of their forgetfulness [of their true nature] and tells them they are in need of enlightenment.... Of course, other sages in the ancient world gave similar advice."

64

One of the scholars writes:

"[Thomas] derives its material not from the canonical gospels, but from the same *oral* traditions on which these [New Testament] gospels themselves rely."

And:

"The 'wisdom' one finds in Thomas is hardly conventional. In fact, if one is to recognize any common wisdom at all in Thomas' outlook, one must first, it seems, cultivate a way of thinking that subverts dominant cultural values…

"The theological underpinnings for Thomas' decidedly counter-cultural bent also go somewhat beyond those of standard Wisdom theology. The truth Thomas reveals about human nature extends beyond the rather ordinary observations that people tend to be selfish, vain, judgmental, foolish, and easily led astray…. Thomas presents us with a Jesus whose words call one from *out* of the chaos into a quest, to seek and to find…

"Even a cursory reading of Thomas will reveal that many of its sayings are quite obscure, some perhaps intentionally so, often using paradox or obtuse metaphors to make their point…. There is still much work to be done before this text is fully understood."

Clues in the binding of the Coptic codices from Nag Hammadi indicate their production around 350–400 C.E. But how early were the Thomas sayings *originally* recorded in the Greek, from which the surviving Coptic text was eventually copied (even assuming the quotations were not initially recorded in *Aramaic*—as were some of the Dead Sea Scrolls of the Essenes, who were contemporaries of Jesus)?

As Pagels says, "scholars sharply disagree about the dating of the *original* texts."

It is significant that, in the Gospel of Thomas, the speaker is simply called Jesus, and not by any celestial names or honorific titles—not even "Christ"; the author of the original collection may never have *heard* of such titles. And the speaker is clearly regarded in his capacity as a teacher (not even called "rabbi," as in the New Testament).

Scholar Steven (or Stevan) L. Davies gives a date for the gospel as early as 50–70 C.E.

John D. Turner also gives a possible date as early as 50 C.E.

And Stephen Patterson states that, "Thomas could have been assembled any time after the origin of the Jesus movement."

Pagels points out that such estimates are of important interest:

> "Professor Helmut Koester came to conclude that the Gospel of Thomas perhaps could be dated as early as the mid-first century—about twenty years after Jesus' death—which would make it the earliest gospel we know, and certainly one of the most important. John Dominic Crossan and others have written books that follow this view, and many people are still engaged in this research."

Richard Valantasis also referred to Crossan's study of the material in Thomas:

"John Dominic Crossan has stratified the Jesus material according to chronology.... The First Stratum, 30–60 C.E., includes...the earliest layer of the Gospel of Thomas...

"It is certain that some of the material of the Gospel of Thomas comes from the First Stratum...

"The (parallel) parables seem to indicate that the version preserved in the Gospel of Thomas comes from the earliest, and least edited, level of the sayings of Jesus."

Also:

"The application of a mid-*second* century C.E. date to the gospel fails to convince: there simply is no evidence for the fully developed gnostic systems in the Gospel of Thomas...

"...its content shows little, if any, evidence of later gnostic mythology and theology."

Were there even such "systems" as Gnosticism or Christianity in competitive existence at the time Thomas was recorded? Thomas' Jesus—and its scribe—give no evidence of knowledge of either sect.

In any case, it is not difficult to accept that the Gospel of Thomas was in circulation before even Paul's writing (c. 50), and was a source for the New Testament gospel authors.

In fact, Crossan—one of the most prominent of the New Testament authorities—has speculated that another of the Nag Hammadi tractates, the *Gospel of Peter*, may have been a source for all four of the New Testament gospels, utilized particularly for their crucifixion and tomb accounts: "[*Peter*] is earlier than, and independent of, the [four] gospels."

He says that "Mark himself used this text, and the other three [Matthew, Luke and John] used only it and Mark for their own compositions."

For one example, *Peter* has:

> "...the heavens opened and two men came down from there, in a great brightness, and drew nigh to the sepulchre. That stone, which had been laid against the entrance to the sepulchre, started of itself to roll and give way to the side..."

Matthew has: "... an angel of the Lord came down from heaven and, going to the tomb, rolled back the stone..."

Crossan says, "there were no [other] versions of this 'empty tomb' tradition before Mark" produced one for Christianity.

The *Gospel of Peter* is thought to have been banned by Bishop Sarapion (339–359 C.E.), a contemporary and correspondent with Bishop Athanasius.

Commonly accepted among New Testament historians, based on various known data, is a chronology which dates Jesus' death to 30 C.E. Also generally agreed is that, as Ehrman has said,

> "scholars have deduced that Mark was written first, and Matthew and Luke, writing in quite separate communities, *used* Mark in composing their own Gospels."

After these first three (called the "synoptic" gospels, because of their intra-sourced similarity, which then appear in the order of Matthew,

Mark, then Luke), John was composed and it appears fourth in the New Testament.

◎

The Gospel of Thomas contains a number of expressions or verses that have similarities to those in the *four* canonical gospels. However, as Gärtner has observed:

> "What is particularly surprising is that there is scarcely a single complete saying of Jesus which is identical with its synoptic counterpart in every detail."

Some scholars have tended to assume that the differences are because the compiler of Thomas amended (or "redacted") New Testament scriptures in order to incorporate denominational deviances. In point of fact, it is entirely possible that just the obverse is true.

The longer that the Gospel of Thomas would have been in circulation, the more likely it is that the subsequent gospels might have utilized it as a source. But even Mark (around 60 C.E.) may contain signs of such "secondary" use.

Thomas' logion 33 contains four phrases, in its two sentences. Mark 4:21 has a version of one of these phrases; Matthew 5:15 has a version of this phrase; and Luke has *two* versions of this same phrase (11:33 and 8:16). In fact, in the latter Luke verse there are parts of *three* of the Thomas logia, which follow one another.

Another example: where Jesus makes the point (logion 89) that the One who created the outside (of the "cup": the body) likewise created the inside (or spirit), Matthew (23:25-26) has this as a polemic involving the scribes and Pharisees, suggesting that the inside of *their* cup is "full of greed."

Luke (11:37-41) goes even further, leading into it with an implied criticism by a Pharisee who notices Jesus didn't wash his hands before eating. As in Matthew, Jesus—in reply—described the Pharisee's cup as "full of greed and wickedness"; he follows this with a phrase similar to Thomas ("Did not the one who made the outside make the inside also?"); then he concludes with advice (and a non sequitur) to "give what is inside [the cup] to the poor, and everything will be clean for you"!

In a similar example, Jesus in logion 78 appears to be referring to himself, as a man not "clothed in fine garments"—unlike those who "are unable to discern the Truth." Matthew's construction (11:7-10) renders this as "about John," the Baptist, and its use is to praise him as "a prophet." Luke (7:24-27) has the same account as Matthew.

Interestingly, the only specific reference to John the Baptist in all 114 verses in Thomas (logion 46) concludes with Jesus saying that whoever "comes to be a child" (childlike: guileless) "will be acquainted" with "the kingdom" and "will become superior to John."

A phrase from *this* verse follows the logion 78 parallel, in both Matthew and Luke; but now the *conclusion* is that whoever "is least in the kingdom of *heaven*" (in Matthew; "the kingdom of *God*" in Luke) "is greater than" John.

Not only is the New Testament's construction "the kingdom of God" not found in Thomas, it is additionally clear that in this gospel Jesus'

"kingdom" is not a celestial retreat for privileged souls after death, nor to be established only after "the Second Coming of Christ."

In Thomas, the sense of the kingdom is one which is circumstantial or situational; or, more directly, experiential or attitudinal: this is a kingdom which Jesus urges his listeners to partake of *here* and *now*, as if it were an ever-present realm or domain.

He speaks of this kingdom as being "near" or "far," in verse 82, according to how one responds to his message. He advises, "find the kingdom," twice; once adding, "for you are from it." (27 and 49).

Not only find it, but "enter the kingdom" (said four times: 22, 99, 113, 114), as *this* kingdom "is spread out upon the earth" (113). It is not only to be discovered in the external realm "outside of you," but equally "inside of you" (this gospel's third verse).

Valantasis took note of this emphasis in verse 3:

> "...Jesus directs the readers to understand their own empowerment: the 'imperial rule of God' is found both within and without the seeker. True 'leadership' directs the seeker inward to a new understanding of the self, and outward to a new understanding of the world in which God's imperial rule is manifest. The seeker guides the self into knowledge, requiring no external guidance other than the sayings of Jesus that directs seekers to themselves.

> The important point is not only that there is a new understanding of an empowered self, but also that God's imperial rule must be understood anew. The location of God's imperial rule is not in the heavens, nor is it under the earth..."

The Encyclopedia Britannica remarks:

"Since God's power is omnipresent, Jesus may have seen 'the kingdom,' in the sense of God's *presence*, as being especially evident in his own words and deeds.... These other ways of viewing the kingdom do not, however, dominate the teachings of Jesus in the *Synoptic* Gospels."

Perrin sums the matter up most succinctly:

"[The Kingdom of God]is not a *place* or community ruled by God; it is not even the abstract idea of reign or kingship of God. It is quite concretely the activity of God..."

And similarly, the *New Testament's* "Father" (which evokes a patriarchal God dominating the heavens) carries the sense in *Thomas* of Jesus' *source* of gnosis or revelatory inspiration—impersonal and universal; the Eastern word Brahman or Self could be used, if some of Thomas' verses were sprinkled into the sutras.

If you do not... find the kingdom... you will not see the father. (27)

I was given some of the things [e.g., revelations] *of my father.* (61)

Blessed are they who... have truly come to know the father... (69)

... who have heard the word of the father and have truly kept it. (79)

Yet, when Jesus merely refers to "the kingdom" in verse 107, this becomes the "Father in heaven" in Matthew 18:10-14. And in Luke 15:3-7, "kingdom" has been omitted, in favor of a moral about repentant sinners "in heaven."

This embroidering of terms has not gone entirely unnoticed by Biblical scholars. According to Steven Davies,

> "It is Thomas' peculiar trait to use *kingdom* in place of the term *wisdom*; peculiar, of course, in the sense that this is never the New Testament's inference for kingdom."

Bertil Gärtner gives relevant details of its usage:

> "The kingdom of the Father is never used in the New Testament as a definite description: instead 'the kingdom of God' is the commonest term. This term is not found at all in the Gospel of Thomas. Nor is it usual in the New Testament to refer merely to *the* kingdom, as is the case of the Gospel of Thomas. It is, however, evident that this gospel seems to use the various terms denoting the kingdom in such a way that they do not coincide with the New Testament."

Jesus, in speaking to Jews, would have avoided using the name of God; while the gospel authors and Paul, addressing a Greek audience of "pagans," used it freely.

As in the unification of the inside and the outside of "the cup," Gärtner noticed that Jesus said one will enter the kingdom "when you make the inside like the outside and the outside like the inside," in verse 22. That Jesus' kingdom is neither exclusively "here" or "there" undermines *dualistic* notions and suggests the *unity* to be found in Jesus' realm.

Gärtner:

> "In Logion 3, we encountered a strange expression which led our thoughts to the idea that the kingdom was incomprehensible in human categories: i.e. ...the kingdom is within you and it is

outside you. That this expression is linked with the kingdom may be explained by the fact that one of the characteristics of the kingdom is unity, which is over and above all contradictions and is neither the one nor the other."

Elaine Pagels observed,

> "....according to the *Gospel of Thomas*, Jesus ridiculed those who thought of the Kingdom of God in literal terms.... That *Kingdom* then, symbolizes a state of transformed consciousness..."

Bart Ehrman makes similar comments on this subject:

> "In this gospel, Jesus does not talk about the God of Israel, about sin against God and the need of repentance. In this gospel, it is not Jesus' death and resurrection that bring salvation, and there is no anticipation of a *coming* Kingdom of God on earth."

And:

> "Because salvation here is completely spiritual...the kingdom of God is no longer understood as a physical entity, but a *spiritual* one."

This kingdom, he says, "is not a *physical* place outside the person, but a salvation of 'oneness,' of *unity* with the *divine realm*."

And Richard Valantasis:

> "Self-knowledge reveals the connection to the Father; not as an external 'adoption' by a distant heavenly Father, but as 'children of the living Father,' a Father who is *present* and vital."

Therefore, the "kingdom of heaven" that the Jesus of the sayings speaks about (only in three verses) is a condition or state which a seeker can find and enter, be "acquainted" with—because it is not located "here" alone or "there" alone, and is not only "spread out upon the earth" but "inside of you" in the same moment.

In the East, it would be the "kingdom of bliss," the realm of Pagels' "transformed consciousness" and Ehrman's "oneness with the divine." To an enlightened teacher, this would be the only "heaven" that a person need know as real and yearn to seek, wherein one can end divisiveness immediately in one's present experience.

In a similar fashion, the New Testament's use of the term "Son of Man" as a variation on the phrase Son of God is a developed construction; nowhere in Thomas is Jesus said to be the begotten son of God.

Patterson points to the research of both Helmut Koester and Norman Perrin:

> "Koester has argued that the relative antiquity of Thomas may be seen also in its use—or lack of use—of christological titles. Koester argues that in contrast to other documents from Nag Hammadi, Thomas exhibits a singular lack of any use of the christological titles 'lord,' 'messiah/Christ,' or 'Son of Man,' such as had become widespread in early Christianity as early as the Pauline writings and the canonical gospels....

> "Perrin argues that none of the apocalyptic Son of Man sayings may be attributed correctly to Jesus; all derive from the later preaching of the early church."

◎

A few more instances of doctrinal layering are significantly instructive.

Jesus tells his followers, in logion 14, that their commission when visiting outlying communities is to "heal the sick among them." Luke (10:8-9) tacks onto that "and tell them the kingdom of God is near you."

Jesus says (logion 39) that the scribes and Pharisees have "hidden" the "keys of knowledge (gnosis)," having not partaken of it or allowed others that opportunity. Matthew conveys this (23:13-14) as a statement about the Pharisees' not entering "the kingdom of heaven."

Thomas' verse number two is a declaration by Jesus that seekers will be finders, and as a consequence of their astonishing discovery "will rule over the All." Matthew has Jesus merely assure that he who seeks will find. (7:7-8)

Jesus makes a remarkable statement in the context of the nondual teachings, in logion 72:

> A man said to him, "Tell my brothers to divide my father's possessions with me."
>
> He said to him, "O man, who has made me a divider?"
>
> He turned to his disciples and said to them, "I am not a divider, am I?"

Only Luke records this direct teaching by Jesus to his disciples. But not without notable changes: Jesus now says he is not a "judge" and proceeds to give a warning about "greed." (12:13-15)

◎

Such changes are not without striking importance, insofar as Jesus' teachings are regarded by churchgoers today.

Logion 13 is a lengthy and meaningfully instructive passage, in which Jesus queries Peter, Matthew, and disciple Thomas on their perception.

Compare me to someone and tell me whom I am like.

The answers of both of the first two are ignored by Jesus; only Thomas is approved for his answer.

What does the Gospel of Matthew make of *this*? In verses 16:13-20, Jesus is no longer "me" but now designates himself "the Son of Man." (Only once in the entire Gospel of Thomas does Jesus say "son of man" and it is clearly not titular, but means "this person." Logion 86.)

And now the three named disciples are an unidentified "they". Only Peter is named, and his answer is given: "You are the Christ, the Son of the living God." In the Gospel of Thomas, this was his inadequate answer: "You are like a righteous angel."

In the Gospel of Matthew, Jesus acknowledges Peter's accolade, as revealed "by my Father in heaven." Jesus then takes *this* occasion to build "my church," giving *Peter* "the keys of the kingdom of heaven."

This scriptural departure from logion 13 is quite a development for the foundation of the Christian church!

For anyone who compares Thomas' sayings to those that appear in the New Testament, there is ample reason to ponder, as does Ehrman: "Is it possible that Thomas presents a more accurate version of the sayings...that is a closer approximation to the way Jesus actually *said* them?"

◎

While much has so far been said about the authorship of Thomas, a few *relevant* facts need to be considered about the canonical ("Authorized by the church as divinely inspired") sources. A major reason why the indicative significance of the Gospel of Thomas is so little comprehended by the public is that relatively few people really *know* much about the Bible itself.

Bart Ehrman, who has had much to say that is instructive on this point, knows as a professor that

> "...many people today do not know a lot about the New Testament, including such basic facts as what books it contains, when they were written, by whom, when, and for what purpose; how the books were copied and transmitted down through the ages; and when and why they came to be collected together into a canon of Scripture...

> "We don't have complete *copies* of the New Testament until the 4th Century, 300 years after the books themselves were written.... We do not have the *original* texts of *any* early Christian book...The first full manuscript of the entire New Testament... [dates] from the *second* half of the 4th Century. *Most* of the manuscripts we have date from the Middle Ages...

> "Strikingly, no two of these copies, except for the smallest fragments, are exactly alike in their wording. No one knows how many differences of wording there are among these manuscripts. It is safest to put it in comparative terms: There are more differences

among our manuscripts than there are words in the New Testament.

"When was this New Testament finally collected and authorized? The first instance we have of any Christian authority urging that our current twenty-seven books, and only these twenty-seven, should be accepted as Scripture occurred in the year 367 CE, in a letter written by the powerful bishop of Alexandria (Egypt), Athanasius. Even then, the matter was not finally resolved, however, as different churches, even within the orthodox form of Christianity, had different ideas—for example, about whether the *Apocalypse of John* could be accepted as Scripture (it finally was, of course), or whether the *Apocalypse of Peter* should be (it was not); whether the epistle of *Hebrews* should be included (it was) or the epistle of *Barnabas* (it was not); and so on. In other words, the debates lasted over three hundred years."

These accepted, "canonical" twenty-seven books were authored by at least fourteen different sources. The last of these composed was *2 Peter*, "probably written sometime around the end of the first and beginning of the 2nd century..."

"In sum, the New Testament is a much-varied and intriguing collection of books, with different authors, different genres, different audiences, different agendas, and different teachings."

In other words, these are not random anecdotes in the four gospels, they are differently (and deliberately) positioned segments intended to reinforce each author's varied trajectory.

Additionally, says Ehrman, "It seems probably that none of the Gospels was actually written by one of Jesus' closest followers."

This is rather startling when you consider that, as Johnson says, "If the canonical Gospels did not exist, it would be impossible to construct an account of Jesus' ministry." Besides the *apocryphal* gospels, there is no *other* source for an account of either Jesus' deeds or words.

Ehrman points out that, in any event, both disciples John and Peter "are said to be 'illiterate.'" (In Acts 4:13, this is translated in the New International Version, from the Greek, merely as "unschooled".)

Authors of two of the four New Testament gospels would not have been disciples, even at best. Mark was said to have been a later companion of Peter, and Luke a companion of Paul—who himself never met the living Jesus.

But further yet, says Ehrman, all four gospels: "are anonymous writings—only in the second century did they come to be called by the names of Jesus' disciples…"

And:

> "Other gospels appeared that also claimed to be written by apostles. In addition to our newly-discovered *Gospel of Judas,* we have gospels allegedly written by Philip and by Peter; two different gospels by Jesus' brother Judas Thomas; one by Mary Magdalene, and so on."

Regardless of their authorship, Ehrman remarks,

> "These books were not written as dispassionate histories…their authors were *not* eyewitnesses to the events they narrate, but were writing several decades later—telling stories that they had *heard*; stories that had been in circulation year after year, among the followers of Jesus."

80

Not only were these texts not chronicled by witnesses to the events (and "they don't claim to be"),

> "Even if they were *based* on eyewitness testimony, they would not necessarily be historically accurate...

> "The books seem to have been written thirty-five to sixty-five years after the events they narrate, by highly-educated, Greek-speaking Christians (unlike the lower-class, Aramaic-speaking disciples of Jesus). As two of the authors admit, they inherited the stories from the oral tradition."

Luke Timothy Johnson notes of these "acute" questions of "diversity" in the accounts: "John and Matthew are both *supposed* to be eyewitnesses, yet their Gospels are least alike!"

And: "It is true that eyewitnesses can have different perspectives and versions, but the linguistic pattern does not *fit* that of eyewitness *behavior...*"

Johnson also points out, "About ninety percent of *Mark's* material is found in *both* Matthew and Luke". And that those two may either "have independent sources—or *compose* distinctive material..."

In fact, while two of the four books (Mark and John) begin with Jesus at age thirty, the stories *prior* to that time (in Matthew and Luke) have principally been discredited by New Testament historians, as composed for doctrinal purposes.

James Tabor is Chair of the Department of Religious Studies at the University of North Carolina at Charlotte. With a Ph.D. and thirty years of biblical research, he participates in on-site archaeological excavations in Israel. He states:

"It is impossible to write a full biography of Jesus' life. According to the more plausible reconstruction of the chronology, Jesus died at age thirty-three. We are missing any historical record of the first thirty years of his life…

"Mark begins his story with Jesus at age thirty. By chapter eight, more than halfway through his sixteen chapters, he has already come to the final weeks of Jesus' life…

"John begins with Jesus at thirty, and he likewise devotes half his book to his final days in Jerusalem."

A further question of reliability (considering the heavy dependence of the books of Matthew and Luke on Mark) is that, according to Patterson,

"…by the end of the second century, there may have been as many as five different versions of the Gospel of Mark circulating among various early Christian groups."

Were the two *later* writers even consulting the *same* version of Mark?

Then, too, even *if* Jesus' teachings *were* recorded by disciples Matthew or John, or transmitted by Peter through Mark, how thoroughly did *they* comprehend his message?

An interesting progression, concerning this, can be observed. In the book of Mark, in at least a couple of places, Jesus remarks on the lack of perception of the disciples: "Are you so dull?" (7:18); "Do you still not see or understand?" (8:17)

But by the time of the Matthew composition, Johnson says that the disciples "are portrayed as intelligent and understanding students." At 13:16, Jesus now says "blessed are your eyes because they see"; and at 13:51 when Jesus asks, "Have you understood all these things? 'Yes', they replied."

In at least five places in the Gospel of Thomas (alone), Jesus has to clarify to his followers his true nature, in comparison to his earthly *appearance,* "to say that what they seek is already before their eyes," as Davies states, "if they can but see it."

And when Jesus tests the perception of Thomas, Peter and Matthew, in logion 13, "Jesus does not deny what Peter and Matthew have said, but implies that their answers represent inferior levels of understanding," observes Pagels.

Specifically says Meyer of disciple Thomas, "he, and not Simon Peter or Matthew, has the most profound insight into who Jesus actually is."

Jesus saw himself, as did Thomas, as something other than merely a limited physical form. As Valantasis puts it, "he did not understand himself to be a philosopher, an angel, *or* a teacher."

Johnson comments, "The Sermon on the Mount, in Matthew's Gospel, is not Jesus' sermon, but one that has been constructed by Matthew." And Johnson notes that in Mark, "The only human character who recognizes [what the apostles later consider to be Jesus'] true identity is his executioner" (15:39; the centurion somehow knows the preferred designation is "the Son of God"). And there's not even *this* lofty recognition in Luke (23:47).

As for John, his account overall has so little similarity to those before him, that Matthew, Mark and Luke are called "synoptic" because their renditions are so nearly synonymous. As Johnson says,

> "Among the canonical Gospels, *John* is the most distinctive, yet if we tried to place it in the context of the Nag Hammadi collection, it would be *as out of place* as would be the Gospel of Thomas put in John's place."

The major reason for the book of John being considered so "distinctive" that it seems to be an extremity is because it is so heavily laden with Christian rhetoric purporting to spring from Jesus' lips. As the Encyclopedia Britannica phrased it, "Jesus employs long metaphorical discourses in which he himself is the main subject." In a red-letter edition of the New Testament, for example, the whole of chapters 15 and 17 are in red (signifying Jesus' direct quotations).

D. Moody Smith says, of this fourth gospel, that whatever body of Jesus' sayings "as has existed, has been subjected to thorough-going re-interpretation."

And says Norman Perrin,

> "...as far as our present knowledge and methodological resources go, the gospel of John is *not* a source of knowledge of the teaching of Jesus. It is generally recognized that it represents a *reinterpretation* of the ministry and teaching of Jesus along markedly *theological* lines..."

Richard Valantasis compares Thomas and John, through two earlier scholars:

"Helmut Koester has convincingly argued that these two gospels share a common tradition which they interpret in very different ways; while Gregory Riley is persuasive that the communities represented by Thomas and John were communities in a competitive relationship."

But of the two, "the Gospel of Thomas has material that comes from the earliest traditions of the sayings of Jesus ... "

The most striking difference, he suggests, is that salvation has become a promise for the *future* in John, an immediate possibility in Thomas.

That early Christianity was merely a revised form of Judaic apocalypticism can be seen in how heavily the New Testament writers (Paul included) depended upon quotations from the Old Testament —particularly prophecies; Matthew is pitifully dependent, and the whole of the crucifixion and resurrection drama is based on such.

Patterson:

"It is not at all insignificant that the synoptic gospels have preserved the sayings tradition only by embedding it in a biographical framework that presents Jesus as the suffering martyr, marching slowing and deliberately to his death on a cross. Martin Kähler's dictum that the Gospel of Mark is nothing other than 'a passion narrative with an extended introduction' has not yet outlived its usefulness."

Perrin has looked closely at the synoptics:

"The most one could argue is that the [narrative] order presented in early Christian preaching was the result of historical reminiscence; but this is to make an assumption about early Christian preaching; that it was *interested* in historical reminiscence, for which we have

absolutely no evidence. The opposite view, that it was theologically motivated, is the one for which we *have* evidence. The characteristics of the Markan order, and the order of early Christian preaching, are precisely the things that we can explain theologically, whereas it is doubtful whether they are, in fact, true historically....
...what is true for Mark, is true also for Luke and Matthew. They, too, are theologically motivated in the arrangement, presentation and even formulation of their material."

And:

"Any and every saying in the gospels could be the product of an evangelist or transmitter of the tradition. Nor can we *assume* that the sayings will be based upon genuine sayings of Jesus. Mark 9:1 is not, and both Matthew and Luke simply use the saying before them without concerning themselves as to its origin, and the saying they use is, in fact, a Markan production....

"In the case of Mark 8:38, we know that Mark has not composed the saying itself, because it is part of a tradition with a very complex history; rather he has modified a saying, in the tradition, to make it suitable for his purpose. In this respect, Mark 8:38 is like Matt. 16:28 and Luke 9:27, where we can see the theologically-motivated work of the evangelists because we have the earlier forms of the sayings upon which they worked....

"The only man, whose work we can trace in the synoptic tradition, who ever concerns himself to remain reasonably true (in our sense of that word) to his sources is Luke, and even he does not hesitate to make very considerable changes indeed when he has theological reasons for doing so..."

It is in light of such factors concerning the canonical gospels that the Gospel of Thomas needs to be seriously considered.

Patterson has made such a case:

> "However flawed the synoptics may be as pure history, their view of Jesus as an apocalyptic preacher with a mission to Israel, who thought of himself as a Messiah and reflected upon the significance of his inevitable death, has held a rather firm grip on scholarship at least since the days of Schweitzer. But the Gospel of Thomas, building upon that same bedrock of tradition, presents us with a view of Jesus that is quite different.... Thomas and the synoptic gospels, in a sense, represent two diverging trajectories moving out and away from a common beginning in an early Jesus movement grounded in the legacy of Jesus' sayings or words...

> "While work to date has tended to make use of Thomas only when it could be seen to confirm what is already suspected about Jesus on the basis of *canonical* materials, such a limited approach does not tap the full potential of the Gospel of Thomas for the question of the historical Jesus...

> "For even though most modern scholars have come to realize (through the work of Wrede, Schmidt, Bultmann and others) that the synoptic gospels are in no way to be seen as biographies of Jesus, there has nonetheless grown up around them a kind of normative status for the historians...

> "I would stake a rather firm claim: no new quest of the historical Jesus can proceed *now* without giving due attention to the Thomas tradition. As an independent reading of the Jesus tradition, it provides us with a crucial and indispensable tool for gaining critical distance on the *synoptic* tradition, which has so long dominated the Jesus discussion."

So, it is worthwhile then to look at what appears to be add-on theology (in terms of the development of the New Testament's persistent Christian "hereafter" thesis) as it pertains to Thomas' enlightenment teachings.

Nowhere are the programatic differences between Thomas and the four gospels in clearer relief than in the rendering of the few parables which appear in both.

All together, there are considered to be eleven parables in Thomas; ten of these appear in Matthew; seven in Luke; and only three in Mark, the earliest and briefest of all four New Testament gospels. Only three of the Thomas parables appear in all three of the synoptics.

Patterson says that,

> "...since the work of Jülicher, it has long been generally recognized that there is a tendency within the tradition for parables to be *transformed* secondarily into allegories, in the interpretive work of the early *church*. Most of the parables were not originally *intended* as allegories. Second, while the tendency to allegorize appears to have been prominent in the *synoptic* trajectory, in the Thomas trajectory, for whatever reason, this was *not* the case. Therefore, one relatively easy way to begin to isolate the *interpretive* effort, underway in the synoptic trajectory, is simply to hold its allegorized versions of the parables up against their non-allegorized Thomas counterparts."

And he refers to Joachim Jeremias' study, which included,

> "...all of the parables found in Thomas. Jeremias' work is distinguished by the fact that here, for the first time, a major form-

critical study of the Jesus tradition makes extensive use of the Gospel of Thomas as a tool for piecing together the history of the transmission of this material, and ultimately for assembling what Jeremias takes to be the *original* proclamation of Jesus. *Often* Jeremias judges the Thomas version of a parable to be more original than its synoptic counterpart. He frequently contrasts the *simpler* Thomas parable to the synoptic version, to illustrate the tendency of the synoptic tradition to *embellish,* allegorize, to incorporate allusions to the Septuagint and other popular lore, and other secondary features."

If the author of the book of Mark had actually *been* Mark, he would have been quoting Peter, who had walked with Jesus. At Mark 4:34, "He did not say anything to them without using a parable. But when he was alone with his own disciples, he explained everything."

The author of the book of Matthew—a disciple who also walked with Jesus—says (15:15-16):

Peter said, 'Explain the parable to us.'

'Are you still so dull?,' Jesus asked them.

According to Gärtner:

"In the teaching parables of Mark 4, Jesus shows that the parables have a meaning which cannot be comprehended by anyone who does not possess the key to their understanding..."

Evidently, this wasn't the key that Peter, and some of the others, received. So, it's not too surprising how some of these parables were rendered in the New Testament, in comparison with their form in Thomas.

In Thomas' logion 65, "a good man who owned a vineyard" twice sent a servant to the "tenant farmers," who "leased" the land, to "collect the produce."   Both times the servants returned empty-handed after receiving a beating. The owner decided he'd better send his son, and the son was killed.

Reading it objectively, the point of the parable appears to be that when "servants" (or disciples) are sent out into the world to carry the "good man's" message, they may meet with severe hostility.   The parable concludes, "Let him who has ears hear."

In Mark (12:1-9), the owner sent "many" servants, and more than one were *killed* by the tenants.   Despite knowing this possible deadly outcome beforehand, Mark says the owner now sent the "one left to send, a son, whom he loved…. So they…killed him."

Mark proceeds with an ending to the parable that is not found in Thomas: Therefore the owner "will come and kill those tenants, and give the vineyard to others"—which, of course, he could have done after they killed the first of his servants; nor will replacing tenants assure him that he will receive future produce.

Matthew renders the same version as Mark, but Jesus concludes by spouting a judgmental condemnation of Pharisees (21:43); "Therefore I tell you that the kingdom of God will be *taken away* from you and given to a people who will produce its fruit."

◎

Thomas' logion 64 is a parable about a "master" who prepared a "dinner" and then invited "guests" to partake of his offering. The four who were invited were each too busy with commercial interests to share the host's meal. So the host invited, from out on the street, whoever was not so committed to come in and "dine." Jesus then ends with this admonishment: "Businessmen and merchants will not enter the places of my father."

Luke (14:15-24) precedes his version of the parable with a phrase about "the feast in the kingdom of God." Luke's host then, when rebuffed by those invited, "became angry." The parable then concludes with what appears to be an emasculated ending from Thomas: "I tell you, not one of those men who were invited will get a taste of my banquet."

Matthew's entry (22:1-14), like Luke, has turned it into a "banquet," now of no less than "a king" who had butchered his "oxen and fattened cattle." Not only did the invited guests "pay no attention" and "refused to come," some "seized his servants … and killed them."

The "enraged" king "sent his army and destroyed those murderers and burned their city."

So, again, people from the streets were invited in, we're told, "both good and bad." Not surprisingly, the king noticed that one of the attendees was not properly dressed for a banquet, and confronted him: "how did you get in here …"

The king ordered his minions: "Tie him hand and foot, and throw him outside, into the darkness …"

This parable's moral? "For many are invited but few are chosen"!

All of this, remember, is purported to be words spoken by Jesus.

Crossan observes:

"I consider that all of this is Matthew's own composition, a creative addition to interpret the parable according to his own particular vision of its meaning."

And Perrin concludes:

"There is no allegory at all in the Thomas version, and the point is made by a generalizing conclusion which reflects gnostic contempt for the material world and those engaged in its business. It is hard to resist the conclusion that this version is nearer to the teaching of Jesus than either of the others: it does not reflect the situation of the Church, nor, except for the generalizing conclusion, is it at all concerned with anything specifically gnostic."

One of the extrapolations of a parable that most reveals Christian severity relates to logion 8. Jesus described a "wise" fisherman whose net was "full of small fish." Again calling him "wise," Jesus said that among this catch, he "found a fine large fish."

"He threw all the small fish back into the sea and chose the large fish without difficulty. Whoever has ears to hear, let him hear."

Matthew (13:47-50) can't resist beginning this with a phrase about "the kingdom of heaven"; and we now have (plural) fishermen, none of them said to be wise. They *sort* the entire catch, "and collected the good fish... but threw the bad away."

No longer is the parable about astutely cleaving to the one issue that surmounts all others; now it's about the fate of sinners at God's judgement day. "The angels will come and separate the wicked from the righteous and throw them into the fiery furnace, where there will be weeping and gnashing of teeth." Again, these are allegedly Jesus' words.

◎

Lastly, in logion 107, Jesus tells a parable in four sentences, with not one word about "sinners" or "repentance." It is one (of several verses) in Thomas that makes the same point as about the fisherman earlier: a shepherd had a flock of "a hundred sheep." The "largest went astray"; he went to great trouble to look "for that one" until he was certain he had *found* this one of greatest value.

Luke (15:1-7) prefaces the parable with two references to "sinners"; the "lost" now is not the valuable one the shepherd cared most for: the parable has become about, "more rejoicing in heaven over one *sinner* who repents than over ninety-nine righteous persons who do not need to repent."

Norman Perrin sums up such "modification" of the parables, concluding,

> "Most of the parables, however, have been considerably modified in the tradition; they were transformed into allegories, supplied with new conclusions, interpreted and reinterpreted, and always under the pressure of meeting the need of the Church in a *changing* situation. Certainly, every single parable in the tradition has to be approached with the basic assumption that, as it now stands, it represents the teaching of the early Church...not that of the historical Jesus to a group gathered by the Sea of Galilee."

If so with the parables, how much can we trust the gospels' interpretation of Jesus' *direct* statements? Norman Perrin:

"If they [parables] could be so readily and completely *transformed* in the tradition, how much more must (not less strongly) individualistic forms of *teaching* have been transformed?"

◎

It appears that the Gospel of Thomas was known to the early Christian patriarchs who formulated the decision as to which of the many extant gospels would be selected for presentation as the "New" Testament (ostensibly superceding the divine revelation of the Old Testament).

Scholars have a solid understanding of *why* certain gospels were chosen, as opposed to others, based on the preserved writings and letters of the Church "fathers."

There are some books in the New Testament that are so distinctly different from its overall character—for example, the abstruse *Revelation* (and some would say *John*)—that the "sayings" gospel of Thomas would not be conclusively out of place on that basis alone.

But Thomas would stand out starkly on the basis of what it is *saying*, to the seeker of unmediated spiritual unity with the divine, or Absolute.

There was calculated reasoning behind the structuring of the "orthodox" ("conforming to established or approved beliefs or opinions") canon; and it emphasizes the Gospel of Thomas' importance when this is clarified.

Bishop John Shelby Spong has observed:

"'Orthodoxy,' which by definition means 'right thinking', has always assumed a dualistic world divided between nature and supernature, body and soul, humanity and divinity..."

A number of the other noncanonical testaments (or "apocrypha")— some apparently written later than Thomas, and some possibly as early—contain verses, or their variants, that are found in Thomas. This causes one to wonder how so many of them escaped inclusion by the New Testament authors.

It isn't as if Thomas was not in wide circulation. Gärtner says that non-canonical

> "...sayings of Jesus are known—entire or in part—from quotations of Irenaeus, Clement of Rome, Clement of Alexandria, Origen, Hippolytus, etc. Similar sayings, as well as parts of logia from the Gospel of Thomas, are to be found in other apocryphal acts, and in fragments from the *Gospel According to the Hebrews* and the *Gospel of the Egyptians*. A large group of sayings is also known from the Oxyrhynchus Papyri, and a number of logia have been found more recently in Manichæan and Gnostic documents."

Marvin Meyer reports that, according to Bentley Layton,

> "Thomas' mystical message (of salvation through self-knowledge) may have come to the attention of the great preacher of Alexandria, Valentinus, the probable author of *Gospel of Truth* and the founder of the Valentinian school of Gnostic thought..."

And, regarding the Persian prophet Mani (c. 240 C.E.),

> "With the emergence of Mani and Manichæanism, the Gospel of Thomas and the Acts of Thomas were accepted as sacred literature by the followers of that world religion. Sayings from the Gospel of

Thomas are cited and alluded to in the Manichæan Psalm Book and Kephalaia...

"Many years thereafter, the medieval Islamic scholar Abu Hamid Muhammad al-Ghazali cited dozens of sayings of prophet 'Isa in his book *The Revival of the Religious Sciences,* and among them are sayings reminiscent of what Jesus says in the *Gospel of Thomas.*"

And Pagels:

"Certain fathers of the church had mentioned by name such writings as the *Gospel of Thomas* and the *Gospel of Truth,* but apart from the names, such writings had remained virtually unknown, since some of the same church leaders had attacked them as heresy."

Also:

"The renowned Egyptian teacher Origen, writing about a generation later [than Hippolytus] also mentions the *Gospel of Thomas*..." *

What, in fact, makes some of the Library texts so unique is that significant elements of their material has no parallel anywhere in the Bible.

For example, one of the most remarkable self-referential passages of Jesus is given in the five sentences of Thomas' logion 77—particularly the phrasing of the last two sentences (which also appears in other Library texts): "Split a piece of wood, and I am there. Lift up the stone, and you will find me there."

---

* See page 134.

The omnipresent Being that is spoken of here is not going to ascend to Heaven only to later be present again with the Second Coming—which is presumably why it wasn't suitable for New Testament inclusion.

What *was* deemed suitable for inclusion has intrigued scholars.

1 and *2 Timothy* and *Titus*, alleged to have been penned by Paul, are believed by scholars to be forgeries. And *Ephesians, Colossians* and *1* and *2 Thessalonians* are similarly suspected. Likewise, *1* and *2 Peter*, claiming to be written by Peter, are also believed to be forgeries.

The book of *James* does not claim to be written by the brother of Jesus, but it was accepted as such for canonical inclusion. The author of *Jude* claims to be a brother of James, though also not claiming to be a brother of Jesus, but was also similarly accepted to be such. (Jude and James were common names in ancient times, says Tabor.)

And *1, 2* and *3 John* do not claim to be written by the apostle, but were accepted as such.

The Bible's New International Version states, in notes, that the book called *Revelation* "was written by the apostle John." But according to Ehrman, "Scholars continue to believe to this day that the author of the *Gospel of John* and the author of the *Revelation* of John are *not* the same person." So, if John wrote *Revelation*, he didn't write *John*.

The above mentioned represent 15 of the 27 books of the New Testament: 55%!

There was also a *3 Corinthians* in circulation, a forgery that didn't get included in the Bible. Ehrman has put as a question: "How can we explain the presence of forgeries among the early Christian writings? ... would highly-religious, moral people engage in deception?" *

And Gärtner states: "According to Harnack, in the middle of the 2nd Century it was the fashion to alter and forge authoritative texts ..."

Perrin comments, "the gospel form was created to serve the purpose of the early Church, but historical reminiscence was not one of those purposes."

The Gospel of Mark is interrupted halfway through its final chapter, in most bibles today, by a sentence in small type: "The most reliable early manuscripts and other ancient witnesses do not have Mark 16:9-20."

The first *eight* verses, of the conclusion (16:1-8) of this earliest gospel, portrays three women visiting the tomb where Jesus' body had supposedly been taken. All they found there was "a young man dressed in a white robe." He asserts that Jesus "has risen," and that he will be found in Galilee.

The "bewildered" women "fled," and "said nothing to anyone ..."

That is where Mark's author *ended* the account.

But at a later point in the development of the canon, a longer ending was appended.

---

* At another point, Ehrman has seemed to answer his own question, remarking that, in the 2nd Century, church traditions included an account that Pontius Pilate had converted to Christianity.

While the original portion reported only a claim by a young man that Jesus had risen, and the disbelieving women not repeating such a claim to anyone, this has all been amended.

The first verse of the appendix has Jesus "appearing" to one of the three women. She now goes and tells an unnamed group of followers that "Jesus was alive."

Next, Jesus appears "in a different form" to two of these unnamed followers. Then he appears to the remaining eleven disciples (minus Judas), telling them that "whoever does not believe [his revival from the dead] will be condemned."

In a matter-of-fact conclusion, "he was taken up into heaven and he sat at the right hand of God"—as if someone would know the latter.

This is a staggering difference from where Mark's report ended.

Tabor writes:

> "This added ending does not appear in our two oldest manuscripts, Sinaitius and Vaticanus, dating to the early 4th century A.D. It is also absent from about one hundred Armenian manuscripts, the Old Latin version, and the Sinaitic Syriac. Even copies of Mark that contain the ending often include notes from the scribe pointing out that it is not in the oldest manuscripts."

Ehrman, again, has authoritative comments:

> "There is solid evidence that the stories about Jesus were modified over time, before being written in the Gospels, and that, in fact, some of the stories are not historical at all…."

"Of the nearly 5,400 copies of the New Testament writings that survive today (in the original Greek), no two are exactly alike; all have mistakes, to a greater or lesser degree. Some of the changes appear to have been made intentionally by scribes concerned to make the texts say what they were already 'known' to mean, making the texts less susceptible to 'heretical' interpretation and more clearly orthodox. This is a phenomenon that scholars have come to call, somewhat ironically, the orthodox corruption of scripture."

"Some differences have an important bearing on how we understand the Gospels, or how we understand Jesus' message and mission..."

"This kind of alteration of the text sometimes had a permanent affect on Christian interpretation of these texts, because in some cases, it was the *altered* text that came to be copied more than the original text.   Even today, people sometimes base their understandings of the New Testament on passages that we do not *have* in the original wording."

And:

"It is important to remember, when we read the New Testament, that we are not reading the *originals* as produced by the ancient authors. We are reading translations into English of Greek texts, whose originals do not survive; these translations are based on copies of the originals, and all of these copies have errors in them. In some places, we may not even know what an author originally said."

Also, Ehrman says that some of the Nag Hammadi Library treatises "were not Christian in any sense. It is interesting to note that some of the non-Christian texts give evidence of having been 'Christianized' by later editors," as seen in copies of versions dated as later.

Bart Ehrman's research into such matters was published as a *New York Times* bestseller, titled *Misquoting Jesus: The Story Behind Who Changed the Bible and Why.*

The Encyclopedia Britannica summarized the matter:

> "...the Synoptic Gospels are theological documents that provide information the authors regarded as necessary for the religious development of the Christian communities in which they worked....
>
> "This means that the sequence of events in Jesus' ministry is *unknown*. Moreover, the Evangelists and other early Christian teachers also *shaped* the material about Jesus....
>
> "The lack of firm knowledge of original context makes the precise interpretation of individual passages difficult."

The linchpin in the Christianizing of Jesus' teachings was a moralizing evangelist who had never walked with the sage.

The early shadow of Paul was evidently cast over all four composers of the Biblical gospels. "Some have argued that without the apostle Paul, says Ehrman, "Christianity would have been *radically* different."

To him are ascribed 13 of the 27 New Testament books—nearly half! All of his writing appears to have been issued between 50–64 C.E. (he supposedly was executed in Rome around the year 65, though the Bible does not say this).

The Gospel of Mark is generally dated to no earlier than 70 C.E., twenty years after Paul's output was circulating (both Paul and Peter had died, the latter said to be in 63). Matthew and Luke are thought to have been composed not before the year 80, and John not before 90. The book of Acts (believed to have been written by the same author as Luke), which chronicles Paul's proselytizing, may have been penned as much as thirty years after Paul's death.

Says Patterson, "John 'spiritualized' the gospel, and Paul recast it in the form of the syncretistic [organized] Christ cult..."

Tabor observes,

> "Paul's influence within our New Testament canon of documents is *pervasive.* I would go so far as to say that the New Testament itself is primarily a literary legacy of the apostle Paul....
>
> "The book of Acts is almost wholly a defense of his central place as the 'thirteenth' apostle....
>
> "[Mark] is a primary carrier of the message that Paul preached, projected *back* into the life of Jesus. Both Matthew and Luke, who use Mark as their main narrative source, then passed on Mark's core message. The gospel of John, in theology at least, also reflects Paul's essential understanding of Jesus. Paul's view of Christ as the divine, preexistent Son of God who took on human form, died on the cross for the sins of the world, and was resurrected to heavenly glory at God's right hand became *the* Christian message."

The entire New Testament theology, then, appears to have been influenced by Paul's notion that one can only connect with the divine by "believing" that Jesus ascended bodily into the sky—the theme which seems to be the criterion for all the texts that were selected as "canonical".

102

Scholars now generally date Jesus' birth at around 4 B.C., and his death at around 30 C.E. There seems to be nothing in the Gospel of Thomas to demonstrate that its sayings could *not* have been recorded even while Jesus was alive. So, conceivably it could have been in circulation for as much as a couple of decades before Paul's writing began.

One faint echo that sounds like Thomas is where Paul says that "for all sons of God" their is "neither Jew nor Greek, slave nor free, male nor female, for you are all one..." (Galatians 3:26-28).

Actually, there is no reason to believe that Paul knew anything of Jesus except what he would have received as hearsay through the oral sources: not even the *first* of the *gospel* accounts had been written during his lifetime, it appears.

In fact, in his writings he seems to know of only two sayings that Jesus is supposedly accountable for: if married, remain so; and, accept recompense for preaching. He did not demonstrate, in any case, a particular interest or concern about Jesus' activities or promulgations.

For both Paul and the author of John, says Perrin, they

"...require no more of history than the 'that' of the 'life' of Jesus and his crucifixion for their proclamation....

"For this reason, Paul can speak of words from the Lord and mean words possibly originating from Jesus but heavily reinterpreted in the Church, and overlaid with liturgical instructions (I Cor: 11:23-25), because he is completely indifferent as to whether all, some *or none* had, in fact, been spoken by the earthly Jesus. For this

103

reason, the synoptic evangelists can take words originally spoken by Christian prophets (e.g. the apocalyptic 'Son of man' sayings) and ascribe them to Jesus, and can also freely modify and reinterpret sayings in the tradition to make them express their own theological viewpoint (e.g. Mark 9:1) and still ascribe *them* to Jesus."

◎

2 *Peter* 3:15-17 says of "our dear brother Paul" that

"His letters contain some things that are hard to understand, which ignorant and unstable people distort—as they do the *other* Scriptures—to their own destruction.   Therefore...be on your guard so that you may not be carried away..."

The crucial difference between the Gospel of Thomas and the New Testament is that the kingdom which Jesus urges his listeners to seek and to enter has no connecting points with an alleged bodily revival *or* a proclaimed elevation as the "only begotten" Son of God.

As Gärtner writes:

"It has already been pointed out, more than once, that the Gospel of Thomas reproduces none of the narrative sections from the canonical Gospels. This can scarcely be explained otherwise than by saying that this has to do with an intense interest in Jesus' *teaching*. In a Gnostic milieu, it is the knowledge mediated by the Savior which is the essential factor; hence Jesus' earthly life and those of his miracles, which have as their object the things of this world, lose interest."

In addition, there is no reason to believe that the compiler of Thomas had any knowledge of what was to become, with Paul, a sectarian Christian embellishment.   As Patterson noticed, "Thomas seems

104

scarcely aware of the tradition in which Jesus' death had become the focal point of the theological reflection."

Of this focal point, Johnson has said, "the Gospels were written from the *perspective* of the resurrection faith…*products* of post-resurrection reflection on Jesus…."

> "The gospels are not composed by eyewitnesses immediately after the resurrection… The main vehicle for transmitting the memory of Jesus, over a period of some forty years, was through oral tradition…"

And Tabor:

> "What we have to realize is that the gospels of Matthew, Luke, and John were written between forty to seventy years after the death of Jesus by authors who were *not* original witnesses and who were not living in Roman Palestine…"

When one considers every disputation about the New Testament, no controversy is greater than the resurrection account.

The author of John does not even portray an ascension of Jesus to heaven, as sensational as that would have been to *his* narrative as well.

Even the account in Mark is acknowledged to be a later filagree, as already mentioned here.

The Encyclopedia Britannica says of the resurrection:

> "It is difficult to accuse these sources, or the first 'believers,' of deliberate fraud…. The uncertainties are substantial; but—given

the accounts in *these* sources, certainty is unobtainable...many details are uncertain or dubious."

Jesus' 'resurrection' is what made Christianity distinct from Judaism. Ehrman:

"Before Christianity, we have no indication that any Jew anywhere thought that the messiah would suffer and die, even for the sins of the world. Not a single reference exists to any such idea in any Jewish text—including the Hebrew Bible—before Christianity."

And:

"Moreover, the sources are hopelessly contradictory, as we can see by doing a detailed comparison of the accounts in the Gospels: Who went to the tomb? How many people went? What were their names? What did they see when they got there? Whom did they meet? What were they told? What did they do as a result? Answers to each of these questions are not only different among the Gospels but also completely divergent."

Bishop Spong has noticed:

"When we go to the details of the resurrection, as found in the gospels, we are confronted with a host of assertions that are contradictory, confusing and baffling....

"... the gospels tell us that a group of women went to the tomb on the first day of the week. Paul has no mention of this tradition. The gospels all do; however, they do not agree on exactly who the women were or what their number was. Mark has three women, Matthew two, Luke five or six, and John only one. No gospel writer agrees with another on this *minor* detail. Did these women see the risen Lord on that first Easter morning? Mark says no; Matthew says yes; Luke says no; John says yes."

Spong adds:

> "Paul, in the earliest New Testament writing we have, asserts that Jesus was crucified. In fact, he refers to the cross of Jesus at least eight times, to Jesus' act of being crucified nine times and to the death of Jesus numerous times." Yet Paul says nothing about a bodily resurrection.

Meyer remarks:

> "Jesus in the Gospel of Thomas is not presented as the unique or incarnate son of God, and nothing is said of a cross with 'saving' significance, or an empty tomb. Jesus is named the living Jesus, but God is also said to be a living one; and followers of Jesus are called living ones as well. Referring to Jesus as the living one, then, is not a specific reference to the resurrection; rather, this phrase indicates all that is part of the realm of life."

Jews would have been looking for a kingly Messiah, Christians for a celestial Savior. Jesus would have likely told all to look *within* for the divine.

As the Encyclopedia Britannica puts it,

> "Although Jesus specifically called several followers, he seems not to have viewed personal faith in and commitment to him as absolute necessities..."

◎

Considering that none of the gospel writers were eyewitnesses to *anything* described, and that even Mark was presumably recording an oral legend that was likely already forty years old, how much "faith" is justified concerning the astonishing resurrection story (or *stories,* since even what we have is not *consistent*)?

But what is the import of this legend for Thomas, which *doesn't* contain such drama? As Patterson says, "it need only be pointed out that this new emphasis on significant *events* in Jesus' life will leave the Gospel of Thomas, which contains almost nothing of biographical significance, languishing on the side-lines."

And the important point for the Gospel of Thomas is that if *Jesus* were to have spoken of a resurrection, it would likely have been of a transformative experience that is contingent upon the entering of his kingdom by anyone.

As phrased by Ethan Walker III,

> "The resurrection is referred to in Hinduism and Buddhism as enlightenment or liberation. It is a dramatic change in one's life and one's perspective."

From the Nag Hammadi Library's *Gospel of Philip*:

> "Those who say they will die first and then rise are in error. If they do not first receive the resurrection while they live, when they die they will receive nothing."

The Gospel of John has Jesus saying, "*I* am the resurrection and the life."

According to Mark (10:15), Jesus held children in his arms, and said that those who don't receive the kingdom "like a little child will never enter it." Would those infants be ones who "believe in the resurrection?"

Also, John has Jesus saying, "before Abraham was born, I am." Is this ageless spirit a subject candidate for a resurrection?

The thrust of the resurrection story is to create a Jesus that can be worshipped as a god, replacing the Jehovah of the Jewish Old Testament, as well as the gods of the Greeks and Romans whom Paul was intent on converting into a new religion.*

This move would be precisely contrary to the perspective emphasized in the Gospel of Thomas.

In Thomas, there is a reference to God in verse 100: "Give Caesar what belongs to Caesar, give God what belongs to God"—and Jesus continues with a distinction—"and give me what is mine."

The word is used again in (the ungarbled version of) verse 30: "Jesus said, 'Where there are three [duality], they are without God"—and again a distinction—"and where there is but a single one [nonduality], I say that I am with him."

---

* It is noteworthy that the Bible says that Paul avoided "preaching the word in the province of Asia" (Acts 16:6). What better territory in which to convert "pagans"? Or did he recognize that his theology would merely be found amusing there?

Also, throughout Thomas, Jesus is not portrayed as anything other than a (mortal) human being. Notice how thoroughly he is depicted as normal in the *Gospel of Philip*, from the Library:

> "...the companion of the (Savior is) Mary Magdalene. (But Christ loved) her more than (all) the disciples, and used to kiss her (often) on her (mouth). The rest of (the disciples were offended)..."

But the essence of Christianity is based on the elevation of a man known as Jesus to a god called Christ.

Again, Bart Ehrman has looked closely at this development. In Mark, Jesus "is portrayed as completely human in every way. He never talks about himself as divine, and no one identifies him as being God—not even Mark himself." In Matthew, "The Son of God is not a divine being."

Luke, writing for Greeks, "is the one that portrays Jesus more in line with what pagans typically thought about divine men."

By the last gospel, John, it was Jesus "who was responsible for the creation of the universe [and] who is called God both by the author and by others in the Gospel..."

For example, in John 10:34, Jesus says he is "the one whom the Father set apart as his very own...I said, 'I am God's Son.'"

Ehrman:

> "By the end of the first century, with the Gospel of John, we know of Christians who called Jesus *God*. This was obviously far removed from what Jesus himself said. Jesus was an apocalyptic prophet of the coming kingdom; the Christians came to think of him as the creator of the universe. It's an astounding difference."

Further, Ehrman concludes:

> "Christians who continued to be convinced that Jesus was a righteous man (but nothing more than a man) would obviously remember his sayings far differently from Christians who believed that Jesus was God himself. The Gospels we have inherited reflect these differences. They do not really all say the *same* thing. As historians, we cannot take any one of these accounts at face value as preserving a portrait of Jesus as he really was. Instead, we need to sift through each of these portraits carefully and cautiously, seeking to determine the words and deeds of the man who stands behind them all."

And so we now have—with the four New Testament gospels, and Paul's epistles prior to them—the core of Christ-ianity, a new religion that was being promoted as the stairway to Heaven for pagan Gentiles.

Since a "pagan" was considered to be, as Ehrman says,

> "anyone who was *neither* Jewish *nor* Christian, we are talking about something like *90-93 percent* of the population of the *empire*…

> "Jesus' followers began to modify his *message* after they came to believe that he had been raised by God from the dead, as they transformed the religion *of* Jesus (i.e., the one he preached) into the religion *about* Jesus…

> "Christianity *uniquely* insisted that *its* understanding of the relationship with God was the only true one; there was no other 'way to salvation'…on a very basic level, the struggles involved what it was that *should and must* be *believed* by those who converted to this faith."

And of course, of the *religious* orientations of his day, "Jesus was aligned with *none* of these groups, and had deeply-rooted differences with each of them," Ehrman states.

But within fifty years of Jesus' death, Matthew's author has Jesus talking about his "church" (16:18 and 18:17).

And by at least 112 C.E., in a letter of Pliny the Younger to the Roman emperor Trajan, there is already mention of "followers of Christ, whom they worship as a God."

But meanwhile, there was a change in one direction: as the Savior failed to return to earth from the celestial realm in a Second Coming, references to the "coming" of the Lord diminish as the New Testament books continue to be composed.

With the establishment of an organized religion, and its churches or temples or mosques, comes the necessity for "caretakers" of the institution, the priestly caste, the keepers of the keys to the Kingdom of God.

And follows also the creation of the category of "heretic," those who've chosen not to be part of the orthodox theological conclave.

Interestingly, the gospels tell us that the cross that is symbolic to Christians is the means by which an unrepentant heretic of his time surrendered his life, at the behest of the religious leaders of his time.

The definition of *apocryphal* is, in part, "various writings falsely attributed to Biblical characters [as were the New Testament gospels], or not included in the New Testament because not accepted as resulting from revelation."

The word *apocrypha* itself means "hidden"; but hidden by whom—its authors, or its critics?

An early scholar, Walter Bauer, took the view, according to Elaine Pagels,

> "that the early 'Christian' movement was itself far more diverse than orthodox sources chose to indicate. So, Bauer wrote, 'perhaps—I repeat, perhaps—certain manifestations of Christian life that the authors of the church renounce as *heresies* originally had not been such at all, but , at least here and there, were the *only* forms of the new religion...'"

And Helmut Koester has said: "Only dogmatic prejudice can assert that the canonical writings have an exclusive claim to apostolic origin and thus to *historical* priority."

What we're concerned with here, in the context of the Gospel of Thomas, is not an inconsequential development.

Of the literally thousands of ancient manuscripts relating to Jesus which biblical historians have examined, it was not until nineteen *centuries* after the sage's *death* that a manuscript of the Gospel of Thomas was to be seen—and then evidently only because some Christian monks had hidden their copy. This is the *only* copy ever to have been discovered anywhere.

Those investigating the new religion, who might have wanted to peruse the Gospel of Thomas (among those relatively few people who even knew of Jesus), were warned to ignore such material.

Even as late as the 2nd and 3rd Century, according to Ehrman, "the world was principally, and almost exclusively, pagan." The Roman *Empire*, at this time, is usually thought to have had a population of around sixty million people—of which something like seven percent were probably Jewish.

By the beginning of the 2nd Century, the Christian population numbered "maybe two percent or three percent." Ehrman estimates, "it's not until the beginning of the 4th Century that Christianity can claim anything like *five percent* of the population."

So, in the earliest stages, there was a very small minority of Paul-influenced congregants, calling themselves followers of "Christ," who were in opposition to those who considered themselves adherents of Jesus.

Paul, in his letter to the "churches" he founded in Galatia: "I am astonished that you are…turning to a different gospel—which is really no gospel at all. Evidently some people are throwing you into confusion and are trying to pervert the gospel of Christ." (Galatians 1:6-7)

The author of 1 and 2 *Timothy* (who claims to be Paul) warns against "the opposing ideas, of what is falsely called knowledge" by which some "have wandered from the faith" (1 *Timothy* 6:20-21).

And:

"Avoid *godless* chatter, because those who indulge in it will become more and more ungodly. Their teaching will spread like gangrene. Among them are Hymenaeus and Philetus, who have wandered away from the truth. They say that the 'resurrection' has already taken place, and they destroy the faith of some." (2 *Timothy* 2:16-18).

James Robinson of Claremont College comments:

> "This view, that the Christian's 'resurrection' has already taken place as a *spiritual* reality, is advocated in *The Treatise on the Resurrection, The Exegesis on the Soul,* and *The Gospel of Philip* in the Nag Hammadi library!"

Similarly, the author of 2 *Thessalonians* (at 2:1-2) urges *that* church "not to become easily unsettled" by any suggestion "that the day of the Lord has *already* come."

The leaders of the newly-founded ecclesiastic institution were apparently concerned mainly about three issues: that "knowledge" (gnosis) was said to lead to "salvation," as opposed to belief in ascension and resurrection; that the egalitarian principles of Jesus' teaching threatened clerical authority; and that Jesus' dismissal of material values undermined the church's economic stability.

Pagels researched such developments for her book *Gnostic Gospels,* and has made the points that follow:

> "Gnostic sources offer a different religious perspective. According to the *Dialogue of the Savior,* for example, when the disciples asked

Jesus "What is the place to which we shall go?" he answered, "the place which you can reach, stand there!" [Heaven is not elsewhere.]

"The Gospel of Thomas describes [unawakened] existence as a nightmare. Those who live in it experience 'terror and confusion and instability, and doubt and division,' being caught in 'many illusions.'

She quotes:

"'This is the way everyone has acted, as though asleep at the time when he was ignorant. And this is the way he has come to knowledge, as if he had *awakened* ... as the darkness vanishes when light appears, so also the deficiency vanishes in the fulfillment.'"

She also quotes from the *Dialogue of the Savior*.

"As Jesus talks with his three chosen disciples, Matthew asks him to show him the 'place of life,' which is, he says, the 'pure light.' Jesus answers, 'Every one (of you) who has known himself has seen it.'

"Here again, he deflects the question, pointing the disciple instead toward his own *self-discovery*. When the disciples, expecting him to reveal secrets to them, ask Jesus, 'Who is the one who seeks, (and who is the one who) reveals?', he answers that the one who seeks the truth—the disciple—is also the one who reveals it ..."

According to the *Book of Thomas the Contender*,

... whoever has not known himself has known nothing, but he who has known himself has at the same time already achieved knowledge about the depths of all things.

Pagels says:

116

"Whoever comes to experience his own nature—human nature ["true nature"]—as itself the 'source of all things,' the *primary reality*, will receive enlightenment. Realizing the essential Self, the divine within, the gnostic laughed in joy at being released from external constraints, to celebrate his *identification with the divine being*:

> "*The gospel of truth is a joy for those who have received, from the Father of truth, the grace of knowing him… For he discovered them in himself, and they discovered him in themselves, the incomprehensible, inconceivable one, the Father, the perfect one, the one who made all things.*"

Luke Timothy Johnson has pointed out elements in several of the gnostic gospels that would have disturbed church patriarchs, including the assertion that "mysteries are revealed to other disciples than the Twelve."

Among *his* interpretation of the *Gospel of Truth*:

> "The 'fall' of humans is a matter of ignorance and forgetfulness…. Such alienation results in envy, strife, and division. The recovery of humans… is a matter of awakening, and regaining sight. The result of 'saving' knowledge is unification…
>
> "Jesus enlightens those who are in darkness, and teaches them the way of truth…. Jesus reveals the truth to his followers about who they *already* are but have forgotten…. Concern for others is expressed through the sharing of saving knowledge. *

---

* The Gospel of Philip: "for if one can't receive, how much more can he give?"

"The image of Jesus and of discipleship in the Gospel of Thomas is distinctive: Jesus is a sage, the revealer of the authentic *self within*; discipleship does not mean 'follow me,' but *'realize* who you *are.'*"

Not only did these noncanonical gospels stress that the connection with the divine is a revelation through self-realization, they also insisted that the 'resurrection' was not a reality for the dead but a potentiality for the living.

Pagels:

"One gnostic teacher (whose *Treatise on Resurrection,* a letter to Rheginos, his student, was found at Nag Hammadi) says: 'Do not suppose that "resurrection" is an apparition [phantasia; literally, 'fantasy']. It is not an apparition; rather it is something real. Instead,' he continues, 'one ought to maintain that the *world* is an apparition, rather than resurrection.' Like a Buddhist master, Rheginos' teacher, himself anonymous, goes on to explain that *ordinary* human existence is spiritual death. But the resurrection is the moment of *enlightenment*: 'It is...the revealing of what truly exists...and a migration (metabolē—change, transition) into newness.' Whoever grasps this becomes spiritually alive. This means, he declares, that you can be 'resurrected from the dead' right now...the *Gospel of Philip* expresses the same view, ridiculing ignorant Christians who take the resurrection literally. 'Those who say they will die first and then rise are in error. Instead they must receive the resurrection while they live'...

"Only those who come to recognize that they have been living in ignorance, and learn to release themselves by discovering who they are, experience enlightenment as a new life, as the resurrection...

"But non-gnostic Christians do not seek: '...these—the ones who are ignorant—do not seek after God...they do not inquire about

God…the senseless man hears the call, but he is ignorant of the *place* to which he has been called.'"

◎

There is also the matter of the apocryphal writings giving an equal voice to the most prominent female disciple, Mary Magdalene. Pagels:

"The *Gospel of Mary* relates that when the disciples, disheartened and terrified after the crucifixion, asked Mary to encourage them by telling them what the Lord had told her secretly, she agrees, and teaches them until Peter, furious, asks, 'Did he really speak privately with a woman, (and) not openly to us? Are we to turn about and all listen to her? Did he prefer her to us?'…"

"Another argument between Peter and Mary occurs in *Pistis Sophia* ("Faith Wisdom"). Peter complains that Mary is dominating the conversation with Jesus, and displacing the rightful priority of Peter and his brother apostles. He urges Jesus to silence her, and is quickly rebuked. Later, however, Mary admits to Jesus that she hardly dares speak to him freely because, in her words, 'Peter makes me hesitate; I am afraid of him, because he hates the female race.' Jesus replies that whoever the Spirit inspires is divinely ordained to speak, whether man or woman."

Johnson says of this text: "Mary Magdalene is given a privileged role; she asks most of the questions." And also, "Philip assigns a particular importance to Mary Magdalene as a *companion* to Jesus."

Pagels:

"The *Dialogue of the Savior* not only includes Mary Magdalene as one of the three disciples chosen to receive special teaching but also praises her above the other two, Thomas and Matthew: '...she spoke as a woman who knew the All.'"

◎

And there was also the issue of the relevance of a church and its hierarchy. For gnostics, says Jay Tolson, Jesus

"was an *avatar* or voice of the oversoul sent to teach humans to find the sacred spark within. This was a view of Jesus that made priests and even churches peripheral, if not irrelevant..."

And Pagels quotes:

"The *Apocalypse of Peter* declares that 'those who are from life... having been enlightened,' discriminate for themselves between what is true and false. Belonging to 'the remnant...summoned to knowledge [gnosis],' they neither attempt to dominate others nor do they subject themselves to the bishops and deacons, those 'waterless canals.'"

And she says:

"Proponents of these diverse views agreed that the divine is to be understood in terms of a harmonious, dynamic relationship of opposites—a concept that may be akin to the Eastern view of yin and yang, but remains alien to orthodox Judaism and Christianity....

"On what counts does the gnostic accuse these believers? First, that they 'do not seek after God'. The gnostic understands Christ's message not as offering a set of answers, but as encouragement to engage in a process of searching; 'seek and inquire about the ways you should go, since there is nothing else as good as this.'

"Yet all the sources cited so far—secret gospels, revelations, mystical teachings—are among those *not* included in the select list that constitutes the New Testament collection. Every one of the secret texts which gnostic groups revered was omitted from the canonical collection, and branded as heretical by those who called themselves orthodox Christians...the orthodox recognized that those they called 'gnostics' shared a fundamental religous perspective that remained antithetical to the claims of the institutional church...

"The bishops drew the line against those who challenged any of the three elements of this system: doctrine, ritual, and clerical hierarchy—and the gnostics challenged them all. Only by suppressing gnosticism did orthodox leaders establish that system of organization which united all believers into a single institutional structure."

As Johnson sums up the *Gospel of Philip*: "The deepest truth is a secret known only to the few, who know *spiritually*. The 'apostolic men' understand only materially."

He makes this point also concerning the *Dialogue of the Savior:*

"The moral stance advocated by the composition is ascetical, with language about taking off and putting on clothing used symbolically for taking off materiality and putting on spiritually."

Jesus' teachings on the relationship of 'security' to spirituality seems to have created the greatest degree of ambiguity in the emerging Christ cult. Such teachings were not even confined to the noncanonical gospels.

In Luke (14:33), Jesus declares, "any of you who does not give up everything he has cannot be my disciple." Jesus even called followers away from their family and livelihoods (e.g., Mark 1:18-20).

Did he mean it *literally* when he said to give up everything, as he had done? When he sent the twelve out to teach (Mark 6:7-9), he allowed them to take a tunic, sandals, and a walking staff; no bread, no bag, no money, not even a change of clothes—as a mendicant completely vulnerable to the 'what is,' taking "no thought for the morrow."

Nor did Jesus ask a wealthy would-be follower to donate his money to the teacher's community; instead he was instructed to give it "to the poor" (Mark 10:21).

This emphasis changed even among the followers of Paul. The book of Acts (4:32 through 5:2) related that the early church congregants "shared everything they had," even money from the sale of their home or lands. However, it was kept within the congregation; and it was apportioned by church leaders ("placed at the apostles' feet").

In addition, as the years passed and it became clear that the Second Coming was not going to transpire during the lifetime of those participating, the sharing of assets began to disappear from Christian practice.

Ehrman has pondered the Church's present-day attitude:

> "Does it seem appropriate to you to re-interpret Jesus' teachings— that a person should give up everything for the kingdom—so that it is no longer required to give up a single thing?"

Patterson says of the Gospel of Thomas:

"Its attitudes toward family life, toward money and property, toward piety, and toward political life are all quite radical. Its ethos may be described as social radicalism."

New Testament scholars today distinguish between the iconoclastic man named Jesus and the idolatrous image depicted as Christ, the latter coming into history after—not simultaneous with—the former. When one considers what these scholars have to say about the *real* Jesus, it is worthwhile to bear in mind that many of these experts have had a lifelong Christian orientation, and yet they have found documents like the Gospel of Thomas to be instructive in their re-appraisal of the New Testament.

Pagels:

> "The research of *this* generation of scholars opened up new questions: could the Gospel of Thomas, for example, possibly be not a late, 'Gnostic' gospel, as many of us first assumed, but, on the contrary, an early collection of Jesus' teaching—perhaps even one that Matthew and Luke used to compose their *own* gospels? Could it be the so-called Q source, a hypothetical first-century list of Jesus's sayings? Is it possible that the Gospel of Thomas might tell us a great deal *not* about heresy, but about Jesus and his teachings? Could this be an early source—maybe even our earliest source—of Jesus' teachings, collected in an unedited, unvarnished form?"

Patterson:

> "The New Quest began where the last quest left off, viz., with the assumption that the gospels as we have them are not historical

accounts, but products of the early Christian preaching about Jesus."

As Valantasis has found in Thomas:

"Since the narrative voice is minimal (often reduced simply to "Jesus says"), the narrator invests the readers with the authority and power to listen and to interpret for themselves; these readers need no intermediary to read or hear or understand the difficult sayings of Jesus that are recorded here..."

"Many thought that they could hear immediately the words of Jesus without the intermediary of the institutional church and its orthodox theologians."

Bishop Spong:

"To put it slightly differently, but more boldly: How many details of Jesus' crucifixion really happened?   Are the details of his death grounded in tradition and interpretation rather than in fact, as are the details of his birth, the number and identity of his disciples and the 'historicity' of the miracle stories? By and large these are issues that institutional Christianity has never raised. I do not plan to dodge them in this quest for the truth about Jesus."

Norman Perrin is another authority who became disillusioned with the biblical accounts after he began studying them more assiduously, "for we *began* our work on the gospel materials with a different view of their nature, and we would claim that the gospel materials themselves have forced us to *change* our minds."

Not given to hyperbole, he has written quite plainly on this subject:

"No understanding of the teaching of Jesus is possible without the recognition of the significance of its original historical context; and the precaution of constantly seeking to discover that context, and to take it into account, is one that is most necessary for us to take....

"It must be recognized that the narratives in the synoptic gospels were created to express the theology of the early Church... It must be recognized, indeed, that there are comparatively few narratives which correspond in any way to events in the ministry of Jesus, and that where such correspondence is to be found, as for example in the baptism or crucifixion narratives, the gospel account has been so influenced by the theological conceptions and understanding of the Church that we can derive little, if any, historical knowledge of that event from those narratives. Even the fact that the baptism or crucifixion are historical events is not to be derived with any certainty from the gospel narratives; it has to be argued on other grounds... it is the fact that the evangelists were able to use the story to serve their purposes that has caused it to be preserved, not an interest in historical reminiscence as such... the modern distinction between historical Jesus and risen Lord is quite foreign to the early Church...

"The absolute identification of the earthly Jesus of Nazareth with the risen Lord of Christian experience is the key, and the only key, to understanding the phenomena present in the New Testament tradition."

And:

"The almost cavalier manner in which sayings are modified, interpreted and rewritten in the service of the theology, of the particular evangelist or editor, is quite without parallel in Judaism...

125

"So far as we can tell today, there is no single pericope [passage] anywhere in the gospels, the present purpose of which is to preserve a historical reminiscence of the earthly Jesus, although there may be some which do in fact come near to doing so because a reminiscence, especially of an aspect of teaching such as a parable, could be used to serve the purpose of the Church or the evangelist...it is no longer self-evident that the *historical* Jesus is, in fact, the central *concern* of Christian faith, and it may no longer be assumed that the major aspect of that faith is to follow the dictates, encouragements and challenges of the *teaching* of that Jesus."

Perrin also remarks:

"The historical Jesus did not demand faith in himself, but at the most in his word, especially in his word of proclamation of the imminence of the Kingdom of God."

And Ehrman:

"The historical Jesus did not teach about his own divinity, or pass on to his disciples the doctrines that later came to be embodied in the Nicene Creed."

The Gospel of Thomas has given modern-day religious scholars an impetus to redirect attention to that sage's spiritual message rather than continuing a morbid focus on the death of the messenger. While that message is not yet clearly understood in terms of its nondual perspective, that there is a distinctive *importance* to the Thomas gospel's message *is*, for a variety of reasons, being understood.

Meyer says of Thomas, "the gospel resembles other collections of wise sayings—*logoi sophōn*, 'sayings of the sages,' as James M. Robinson has termed this genre of literature...."

> "The sayings, coming from the living voice of Jesus, are not what Jesus once said as much as they are what Jesus continues to say....
>
> "The sayings of Jesus in the Gospel of Thomas have a spiritual tone, and mystical overtones; and readers are encouraged to encounter Jesus, and become one with Jesus, by coming to an understanding of his sayings and living a life of the spirit."

And Perrin:

> "So in the case of the historical Jesus there is an understanding of existence (self-understanding, not self-consciousness) revealed in his teaching which challenges us in terms of our understanding of our own existence...
>
> "But if we are to seek that which is most characteristic of Jesus, it will be found not in the things which he shares with his contemporaries, but in the things wherein he differs from them...
>
> "Therefore, if we are to ascribe a saying to Jesus, and accept the burden of proof laid upon us, we must be able to show that the saying comes neither from the Church nor from ancient Judaism...
>
> "[Jesus] as a historical figure, certainly transcended the categories of his own day, and therefore, so to speak, invites consideration in terms of the categories of another day."

Valantasis has taken a close look at the *immediacy* of the Thomas spiritual message:

"The Gospel of Thomas, as a collection of sayings of Jesus, does not purport to be a systematic or even an organized theological tractate...

"It must be made clear, however, that the Gospel of Thomas does indeed present a recognizable and articulated 'theology,' but both the mode and the content of that theology differs from other theological discourses...

"I would characterize this theology as a performative theology, whose mode of discourse and whose method of theology revolves about effecting a change in thought and understanding in the readers and hearers (both ancient and modern)...

"The theology comes from the audience's own effort in reflecting and interpreting the sayings, and, therefore, it is a practical and constructed theology even for them...

"Although the contours of this subjectivity may be generally (and cursorily) described, they cannot ultimately become clear without a careful and close reading of each saying in the context of all the sayings in the collection...

"The new understanding of *self*, encapsulated in this discovery, provides the primary impetus for searching the meaning of these sayings."

"Jesus said" can also be translated in the present tense as "Jesus says." Valantasis observes:

"The 'living' Jesus presents these sayings. The sayings speak not of dead knowledge, nor of ancient knowledge, nor even of eternal knowledge, but a *present* knowledge...

"Thomas' kind of person, alone, hearkens to the days of immediate presence of Jesus without any need to engage in imitation either of Jesus or of the disciples..."

Although Valantasis himself has been an Episcopal priest, his commentary on seven of Thomas' verses is not what one would generally hear from a pulpit:

"Jesus is also constructed as a mystagogue (Saying 17), a revealer of sacred knowledge to seekers, who discloses the mysteries to those who are worthy (Saying 62). This mystagogic Jesus describes himself as the light, the 'all' found in every place, the one who is the origin and destiny of all creation (Saying 77). As a bearer of secret wisdom (Prologue), Jesus is portrayed as a divine figure who not only permeates all life, but enables true vision to occur (Saying 37), and who guides people to the fulfilling of their deepest desires (Saying 51). Moreover, Jesus' presence becomes merged with the seeker's, so that there can be no distinction between Jesus and those who follow him (Saying 108)."

And his understanding of another verse (4):

"The final phrase 'and become one and the same' points toward more than inversion, rather to a process of collapsing opposites (such as old and young, first and last) into one. The distinctions ultimately resolve themselves into a state of non-distinction; plurality and opposites are transformed into some sort of unity."

Concluding:

"Those, in these sayings, who search will find themselves in this socially-transgressive mode that will lead to the overcoming of the opposites, to the unity of self that fulfills..."

"The process of self-discovery, that is, does not remain neutral so that one gains an increment of knowledge or understanding which adorns an otherwise rich life. Rather, the knowledge itself becomes the wealth and its lack becomes poverty..."

If indeed Jesus said the words ascribed to him in Thomas, he was expounding nondualism—as any enlightened sage could surely discern. The dualistic doctrines of the church are not consistent with the sage whose wisdom the Gospel of Thomas preserves: this Jesus was focused on the *one* living reality which is *ever present* in our midst and need only be *recognized* as such.

The Gospel of Thomas does not cast Jesus in the light which the organizers of the Christian church would have likely felt suited their doctrinal purposes: early *Christianity* was little more than a radical revision of conventional Judaism. There are indications that Jesus' actual teachings were a *rejection* of *religiosity* in total; his emphasis was that one connect directly with our cosmic source and hence "take no thought for the morrow" or any other mundane consideration. Such perspective does not configure well with concerns for attention to rituals which earn a future place in heaven (or hell)!

And so the plot thickens when we consider how thoroughly and deliberately the Christian patriarchs suppressed the Gospel of Thomas and other gnostic writings that related to its perspective.

Within two generations of Jesus' death, the letters ascribed to Paul and the gospels later attributed to Mark, Matthew, Luke and John were in circulation, all countering the thematic content of the Gospel of Thomas. By the beginning of the 2nd Century, the leadership of a sin-and-repentance evangelism was beginning to coordinate a proscription of so-called heretical spiritual pronouncements.

Johnson has said:

> "Certainly, in the eyes of those writers of the 2nd century later called 'orthodox' (Justin, Tertullian, Irenaeus, Clement), the teachers and doctrines [the apocryphal writings] described represented a clear and present danger."

Tabor says of Justin (who was martyred in 165 C.E.), a Christian convert who was familiar with gnostic and philosophical teachings:

> "By A.D. 150, intellectually astute Christian leaders such as Justin Martyr, living in Rome, had championed the ideas of Paul and had begun to develop a systematic theological system built around his basic ideas. Paul's triumph, to some degree, was a literary one— that is, his letters and the influence of his ideas as embedded in the New Testament writings, including the gospels, became so persuasive that they came to constitute what was viewed as the only authentic Christianity."

Pagels states that orthodox church leaders "have tended to discourage or, at least, to circumscribe the process through which people may seek God on their own…" "But the Gospel of Thomas teaches that recognizing one's *affinity* with God is the *key* to the kingdom of God."

It was just such teachings which especially irritated Irenaeus, the Bishop of the church in Lyons (now France) around 180 C.E.

Ehrman says, "The heretics that Irenaeus found most dangerous to Christian orthodoxy were the gnostics." He wrote a five-volume critique titled *Refutation and Overthrow of What Is Falsely Called Gnosis.* The volumes covered a lot of "heretical" ground.

Meyer:

> "The gnostics discussed by Irenaeus (and others) constitute a major school of mystical religious thought, in antiquity and late antiquity."

He complained that Gnostics were leading away members of his flock "under a pretense of superior knowledge." And, "They say that it is necessary for those who have received full gnosis to be 'born again' into the power which is *above all things.*" So he urges that all "obey the priests who are in the church," and particularly avoid "those who claim access to secret teaching."

Pagels reports that, by 200 C.E.,

> "Christianity had become an institution headed by a three-rank hierarchy of bishops, priests, and deacons, who understood themselves to be the guardians of the only true faith. The majority of churches, among which the church of Rome took a leading role, rejected all other viewpoints as heresy. Deploring the diversity of the earlier movement, Bishop Irenaeus and his followers insisted that there could be only one church, and outside of that church, he declared, there is no salvation. Members of this church alone are orthodox (literally, straight-thinking) Christians...

> "Irenaeus had insisted that such writings were 'wholly unlike what has been handed down to us from the apostles', and he called those who revered such writings heretics.

> "The efforts of the majority to destroy every trace of heretical 'blasphemy' proved so successful that, until the discoveries at Nag Hammadi, nearly all our information concerning alternative forms

of early Christianity came from the massive orthodox attacks upon them. Although gnosticism is perhaps the earliest—and most threatening—of the heresies, scholars had known only a handful of original gnostic texts, none published before the nineteenth century!

"The first emerged in 1769, when a Scottish tourist named James Bruce bought a Coptic manuscript near Thebes (modern Luxor) in Upper Egypt. Published only in 1892, it claims to record conversations of Jesus with his disciples—a group that here includes both men and women. In 1773, a collector found in a London bookshop an ancient text, also in Coptic, that contained a dialogue on 'mysteries' between Jesus and his disciples. In 1896, a German Egyptologist, alerted by the previous publications, bought in Cairo a manuscript that, to his amazement, contained the *Gospel of Mary* (Magdalene) and three other texts."

A contemporary of Irenaeus, and a Christian convert, Clement of Alexandria also knew of—and opposed—gnostics. (Interestingly, by the 9th Century, he himself was regarded as a heretic.)

He quoted in his writings, at one point, lines that are found in Thomas:

"For the Lord himself, when asked by someone when his kingdom will come, said: 'When the two shall be one, and the outside as the inside, and the male with the female, neither male nor female.'"

Clearly, the nondual meaning of these words was lost on him. Ehrman says that he

"interprets the symbolic Gnostic words 'two become one' to mean when we speak truth to one another—when we agree. The Gnostic 'outside like inside' is interpreted to mean that the soul should be visible through good works. The Gnostic 'male and female are neither male nor female' is interpreted to mean that males and females will be equals in society."

◎

Another contemporary of Irenaeus, Hippolytus, a Christian in Rome, also wrote a "massive *Refutation of All Heresies* to 'expose and refute the wicked blasphemy of the heretics.'"

Pagels says that he quoted "some of the opening lines from...the Gospel of Thomas..."

Also of that era was Tertullian, another Christian convert and polemicist who knew of and scorned gnostics, having been influenced by Irenaeus. That women were the equals of men irked him: "These heretical women—how audacious they are! They are bold enough to teach...!"

And of these heretics as a group, he said: "All of them are arrogant... all offer you gnosis!"

Into the 3rd Century (and the next generation), Origen continued the anti-gnostic drumbeat. He was said to have been a student of Clement of Alexandria.

It appears that during his lifetime (said to be 185–254 C.E.) that the Gospel of Thomas was still in circulation: Origen quotes, in one of his writings, logion 82; "I have read somewhere that the Saviour said... 'He that is near me is near the fire; he that is far from me is far from the kingdom.'"

The pursuit continues into the 4th Century, and next generation, with the Bishop of Alexandria (328–375 C.E.), Athanasius. In his thirty-ninth annual pastoral instructions, he listed the 27 "sacred" books that were to be considered orthodox scripture. This not only effectually created the New Testament as it has come down to us today, it also formed the basis for gnostic and other apocryphal texts to be determined "noncanonical" whether prior to or after 367 C.E.

In addition, says Jay Tolson:

> "The letter ordered all Christians to repudiate an assortment of 'illegitimate and secret' Gnostic texts that Athanasius deemed heretical."

It is of interest that despite the church's effort to confine the "sacred scriptures" to a particular set of books, there are fourteen books that are still rejected by Judaism (and all of these regarded by Protestants as noncanonical), while eleven of these are fully accepted in the Roman Catholic canon.

And, remarks Ehrman,

> "In the Ethiopic Church, the ancient book called the Didascalia is included in the New Testament, although it is not in the canon of most Protestant denominations."

Perrin comments,

> "...no distinction should be made between canonical and extra-canonical sayings. As Koester has shown, they are all part of a living tradition in the Church, and no distinction was made between them at all before the second half of the second century."

135

A contemporary of Athanasius was Epiphanius, Bishop of Cyprus (315–403 C.E.), another who had been influenced by the pronouncements of Irenaeus. He described his encounter with Gnosticism in Egypt (at about the time the monks in St. Pachomius monastery may have been perusing their copy of Thomas), according to James Robinson:

> "For I happened on this sect myself, beloved, and was actually taught these things in person, out of the mouths of practicing Gnostics. Not only did women under this delusion offer me this line of talk, and divulge this sort of things to me. With impudent boldness moreover, they tried to seduce me themselves... But the merciful God rescued me from their wickedness, and thus—after reading them and their books, understanding their true intent and not being carried away with them, and after escaping without taking the bait—I lost no time reporting them to the bishops there, and finding out which ones were hidden in the church. Thus they were expelled from the city, about eighty persons, and the city was cleared of their tarelike, thorny growth."

And later, into the 5th Century, Theodoret, the Bishop of Cyrrhus (in Syria) about 450 C.E., wrote that heretical gospels were influencing Christians—evidently his parishioners; even those "who followed the apostolic [orthodox] teachings..."

> "I myself found more than two hundred such books, revered in the churches of my own (diocese), and collecting them all, I did away with them and introduced instead the gospels of the four (canonical) evangelists."

But even before the time of Theodoret, the emperor Constantine (under the influence of Christianity) ordered that the books of heretics were to be hunted out and destroyed, including pagan texts concerning Jesus. In a (preserved) edict that was issued in 333 C.E., he says of one "enemy of piety" that his "books have been obliterated."

This concerted suppression of "unorthodox" gospels left the world at that time with only one version of the teachings of Jesus—and that was a distorted one.

Ehrman:

> "By the end of the nineteenth century, prior to more recent discoveries, our earliest complete texts of the New Testament were from about the fourth century—that is, three hundred years after the writings themselves had been produced, three hundred years in which scribes of varying temperament and ability copied, and often miscopied, their Scriptures...

> "Moreover, the victors in the struggles to establish Christian orthodoxy not only won their theological battles, they also rewrote the history of the conflict; later readers, then, naturally assumed that the 'victorious' views had been embraced by the vast majority of Christians from the very beginning, all the way back to Jesus and his closest followers, the apostles. What, then, of the other books that claimed to be written by these apostles, the ones that did *not* come to form part of the New Testament? For the most part they were suppressed, forgotten, or destroyed...

> "Thus, we have our New Testament today, the collection of books that has proved more significant for the history and culture of Western civilization than any other, without rival in the West for its social and religious importance."

A matter of interest is how the self-justified orthodox writings of the Church fathers has maintained its influence from the days of Irenaeus onward.

We have, sometime after about 370 C.E., early signs of its effect in the burying of noncanonical texts at Nag Hammadi. Valantasis says that biblical scholars were long aware that such suppressed material might lay hidden:

> "*Suppressed* is the key word here, because these documents were believed to be a cache of heretical and rejected documents, curiously preserved in the precincts of an orthodox Christian monastery at Chenoboskion in the Egyptian desert."

Fast-forward to the discovery at Nag Hammadi, and Irenaeus' bias lingers in the air. What Pagels has written on this point is significant to how Thomas has been interpreted:

> "When an international group of scholars first read and published the Gospel of Thomas in 1959, the primary question in their minds, not surprisingly, was this: what can the Gospel of Thomas tell us about 'Gnosticism'—that is, about 'heresy'? Since Irenaeus and others had denounced such gospels, they assumed that Thomas must not only be a false, Gnostic gospel, but also that, being a 'false gospel', it must have been written later than the 'real' gospels. And since most people agree that Mark's gospel was written earliest, some forty years after Jesus's death, around the year 70, Matthew and Luke about ten years later, and John about 90–100, they assumed that Thomas must be later than any of these, and so they guessed that it dated to about 140 C.E.

> "Further, since they assumed that this gospel was heretical, they knew what to *expect* in terms of content: after all, church fathers like Irenaeus basically had defined—or, some would say, invented—heresy. Irenaeus explains that heretics are Gnostics…

"When the first editors of Thomas' gospel found in it virtually no evidence for dualism, nihilism, philosophical speculation, or weird mythology, most assumed that this just goes to show how devious heretics are: they do not say what they really mean. Many scholars decided that even if they could not find these elements in Thomas explicitly, they must be there implicitly; consequently, some decided just to read them into their understanding of the Gospel of Thomas. Most of the first publications did this; some do even now."

Here is an example of how the orthodox Bishops' taint clings on "even now"; a prestigious New Testament professor at a Divinity School has written, of a very plain teaching parable in Thomas (107):

"The Thomas version does not help us very much. We know from the Fathers, e.g., Irenaeus, that this parable was much used by Gnostics; and, both in Thomas and in the Gospel of Truth, where a version of it is also to be found, it has become so much a vehicle for expressing gnostic teaching that the versions do not help us to reconstruct the teaching of Jesus."

To the church's proscriptive attitude toward the teachings of nonduality can be appended an even later addendum—equally as significant as that regarding the Gospel of Thomas.

Many of the statements recorded of Meister Eckhart (1260–1328) could readily appear as sayings in Thomas.

A German Dominican friar, at age 42 he was given his Order's degree of Master of Sacred Theology, and eventually was appointed Vicar-General for all of Bohemia. In 1311, he was sent to Paris to teach, and then was sent, in 1320, to serve as first professor for his Order in Cologne, "considered by many the ideal priest and scholar," according to poet Daniel Ladinsky. "The works of Meister Eckhart...are perhaps at times even divine revelations."

Another writer on Eckhart, Bernard McGinn:

> "Perhaps no Western mystic has appealed so strongly, or offered so fruitful a conversation, to the great mystical traditions of Asia."

James M. Clark, says from his research, concerning the Being which Eckhart referred to as God: "Eckhart's phraseology certainly suggests that he knows this God by direct personal experience."

From what is recorded of his sermons and from his own writings, it is clear that at one point he was the subject of a spontaneous nondual awakening: and he spoke, in conventional terms, from this standpoint to all of his listeners, both learned and unschooled.

A present-day writer on enlightenment, David Carse (*Perfect Brilliant Stillness*), says of Eckhart:

> "...his writings and sermons speak of the same truth of radical non-duality that mystics and sages, East and West, have always pointed toward...the 'breakthrough beyond God', which for all intents and purposes corresponds with (what is referred to in other traditions as) awakening, enlightenment, or the Understanding...

> "Being, for Eckhart, is Presence—which is one, universal... inasmuch as anything is, it is God... 'Thus God is more intimately present to all creatures than the creature is to itself'...

"At times his sermons, in the language of his day, begin to sound remarkably like the sayings of Ramana Maharshi or Nisargadatta Maharaj..."

And Carse notes that—as it is true persistently for the nondual message—Eckhart said, "the truth I want to speak of is such a kind that only a few good people will understand it..."

Among those who didn't "understand it" were the Church's leadership. Although a Dominican friar had never before been charged with heresy, he was (as Clark states it) "found guilty by the highest authority in Christendom."

Pope John XXII issued a bull condemning 28 "propositions" (teachings) of Eckhart:

"Ignoring the shining light of faith, he planted thorns and thistles in the field of the Church, and was active in raising hurtful briers and poisonous shrubs. He taught much that was calculated to obscure the true faith in the hearts of many; and such doctrines he preached persistently, to simple persons in his sermons, besides publishing them in writing."

Eckhart evidently had not expected his inquisitors to judge him to be in error. Ladinsky:

"Eckhart publicly defended himself in February 1327, stating that he had always believed God was as God said He was—Indivisible."

Clark:

"All that can be said is that he died between the 13th February 1327, on which day he defended himself publicly in the Dominican

Church of Cologne, and the 27th March 1329, when the Papal Bull was issued."

Ladinsky adds:

"The Church condemned and suppressed his work, and probably destroyed a lot of it. In the 1880s, two Latin manuscripts of Eckhart's were found. Since 1980 the Dominican Order has sought to reveal that Eckhart was an exemplary Christian mystic and priest."

Many of Eckhart's statements were not unlike those that the Gospel of Thomas reports were uttered by Jesus, and the appearance of any in a condemnatory papal bull is ironic.

One translator of Eckhart's sermons, Raymond Blakney, wrote:

"He lived on that high level, on the same highlands of the spirit that were disclosed in the Upanishads and Sufi classics. To go where Eckhart went is to come close to Lao Tzu and Buddha, and certainly to Jesus Christ."

Indeed, his words could have been spoken by any of the revered sages, allowing for differences in names for the Absolute. (Each sentence here is a quotation):

Whatever He gave to the Son, He...gave it to me just as much as to Him...I am as certain of this as of my own life.

God's is-ness is my is-ness, neither less nor more.

God does not need first to enter the person...because He is already there...for no one can know God who has not first known himself.

He is everywhere, and everywhere entire...He alone 'is one.'

My eye and God's eye are one and the same... To love as God loves, one must be dead to 'self' and all created things...

By virtue of my birth being eternal, *I shall never die... for in bursting forth* [awakening], *I discovered that God and I are One.*

God is something indivisible, acting in eternity... and thus needs nothing... being the ultimate goal [end, or repose]... *That goal has no path which leads to it...*

It would be incorrect for me to call God a being... If you love God as 'a god'—a ghost, a person, or as if He were something with a form—you must get rid of all that! Love him as He is... formless... in whom there is no duality.

There can be no diversity in the One... He who is one with God is... the same existence.

Eckhart sometimes ended his sermons like this:

If anyone does not understand this discourse, let him not worry about that; for if he does not find this truth in himself he cannot understand what I have said—for it is a discovered truth which comes immediately from the heart of God."

And so, we come back to the beginning: to the monks who were contemplating the words of Jesus, as revealed in the Gospel of Thomas, to the disapproval of the church authorities.

As Patterson says of the church:

"The realization that Thomas... represents a tradition that is both independent of, and roughly contemporaneous with, the canonical gospels would have meant the recognition that early Christian claims about Jesus were quite multiple and diverse."

And Johnson has said of diversity: "A vision that embraces the truth of all traditions is the mark of the Gnostic. It follows that traditional Christianity is false insofar as it is exclusive, and is improved to the degree that it is elevated to a more universal view."

Discoveries during the past century have shown that the first four books of the New Testament ("Gospels") are not the only such accounts of the teachings of Jesus which were written during the same time span. The Gospel of Thomas could as readily have been included along with those of Matthew, Mark, Luke and John. That it was excluded from the compilation of the Christian Bible could have resulted from at least a couple of factors: it adheres to the *teachings* but does not include fanciful *stories*; and, it tends to illuminate Jesus as an enlightened teacher of nondualism, *similar* in principle to Guatama Buddha or Ramana Maharshi.

Pagels remarks,

> "If Matthew, Mark, and Luke had been joined with the Gospel of Thomas instead of with John, for example, or had *both* John and Thomas been included in the New Testament canon, Christians probably would have read the first three gospels quite differently... the Gospel of John helped provide a foundation for a unified church; which Thomas, with its emphasis on each person's search for God, did not."

Ehrman:

"The religion of Christianity is probably best understood as having begun not with Jesus' ministry, his death, or his resurrection, but with the *belief* in his resurrection among *some* of his followers...."

"Even then, not every Christian understood Jesus in the same way. In most instances, the beliefs about Jesus that emerged were far removed from what the man himself was really like...

"We can only imagine what might have happened if things had turned out differently; if different books, such as the Gospel of Thomas or the Apocalypse of Peter, had made it into the Bible..."

And Johnson said of the buried find:

"How would our understanding of Jesus be altered if we still had full versions of such fragmentary Gospels?...

"How does the understanding of salvation change when the 'fall' is thought of in terms of ignorance and forgetfulness?"

Elaine Pagels comments:

"In my own case, the hardest—and the most exciting—thing about research into Christian beginnings has been to unlearn what I thought I knew, and to shed presuppositions I had taken for granted.

"This research offers new ways to relate to religious tradition. Orthodox doctrines of God—Jewish, Christian, or Muslim—tend to emphasize the *separation* between what is divine and what is human: in the words of the scholar of religion Rudolph Otto, God is "wholly other" than humankind. Since those who accept such views often assume that divine revelation is diametrically opposed to human perception, they often rule out what mystically-inclined

145

Jews and Christians have always done—seeking to discern spiritual truth experienced as revelation..

"We have also seen the hazards—even terrible harm—that sometimes results from unquestioning acceptance of religious authority."

Jesus:

Let him who has ears, hear.

COMMENTARY ON VERSES: NONDUAL PERSPECTIVE

The Gospel of Thomas is truly a heretical scripture. This text was accredited to the disciple Thomas presumably because he is the one to whom the Gospel says Jesus revealed deeper spiritual knowledge (or gnosis).

To the text's compiler, obviously it is the specific spiritual teachings of Jesus which are of sole and paramount importance. Nearly 90 of the 114 verses recorded begin directly, "Jesus said".

It is clear that virtually every saying quoted is intended as a guiding or teaching pointer similar in character to verses, for example, in the Vedas. And, from the perspective of nondual awareness, it could be said that there is little of the content that is *not* about the explication of nonduality.

For reasons, then, that become clear, there is no talk of a post-crucifixion bodily resurrection, nor any miracle sagas which one could accept only on faith.

The self-references of Jesus, here, are not to the fleshly person but to the embodied Presence of an enlightened sage or master. And there are striking verses said to have been spoken by him—not found in canonical texts—that make sense only within the context of nonduality.

There have been several translations of the Gospel of Thomas. The one recognized currently as the standard, and the one used here, is that of Thomas O. Lambdin. This can be found in James Robinson's

The Nag Hammadi Library in English (Harper-Collins, S.F.;1990, also available on the internet). The use of this text by many, likely most, religious-studies scholars testifies to an acceptable degree of accuracy in this text as given.

The arrangement of the verses or scriptures, rather than following some ideally logical order, appears to be relatively random. And for someone reading from the perspective of Christian doctrine, they present an enigmatic tapestry.

In order to unlock their liberating nondual message, it is necessary that many of the sayings be taken out of their presented context in order to indicate their overlooked context, solely by which can they be understood to make coherent sense. All 114 of the verses thus can be shown to fit into some relationship with each other (aside from the numerical).

Due to the nuance of many of the sayings, some will be rendered here more than once, or in segmented phrases. Many of the verses require attentive contemplation, as their speaker no doubt intended. There are parabolic phrases which have meanings on multiple levels, and these can merit a second or third reading. The word *light*, just for one example, can be interpreted in several different ways.

The verse numbers are generally cited only the first time a verse is referred to.

Due to the nature of the Gospel text, as translated, a number of the verses were sectioned off numerically in what appears to be an arbitrary manner; on the other hand, there are verses which seem to have been unrelatedly lumped together into a single, long verse; and additionally, there are some that apparently were once connected in an earlier version (cf: 6 and 14). An occasional rendering appears to have the omission of a necessary word or two (45: "For out *of lack* of the abundance...").

Also, there are a few references where it is difficult to know what the original allusion symbolized (7: "the lion"; 19: "five trees", which are apparently five specific elements of the teachings). And, of course some words had multiple uses at that time, as many words do today.

Throughout history, spiritual traditions of all kinds have employed certain designations in common: principal among these are the words "relative" and "absolute." The meanings which these words represent are fundamental to the comprehension of the spiritual message. To understand the second of these two words, one must clearly understand the implications of the first word.

That which is relative, according to a dictionary definition, "depends for its identity on some other thing," and therefore is—as a limited form—"not absolute." (A discussion of "absolute" follows our consideration of "relative.")

Anything, in the entire universe, which we have named (or will someday name) derives its existence—as a separate, definable condition or form—by comparison with what it is not; we say that something is "hot" because it definitely is not "cold." The degree of its "hotness" (e.g. boiling) is in direct relationship to the degree of its "coldness" (e.g. freezing). And the subtlety of each relative term can be dependent upon a comparison with more than just one other thing: for example, the distinctive interrelationships in the triad, Father, Son, and Holy Spirit. We would say that you are uniquely "you" not just because you are not "me," but also because you are not any other person in the entire world.

The point of this is that for even one relative category to achieve being, there *has* to be at least two or more relative categories that "separately" (but co-dependently) *also* assume being. For "right" to exist as a particular condition, for example, we are dependent upon a condition which we perceive to be its opposite: "wrong." This "either/ or"—relative—bias (in our fundamental process of thinking about what we perceive as "realities") is what is referred to in spiritual texts as "duality." This is our customary, habitual, learned pattern of thinking: to think of all things—whether material or immaterial, general or particular—in a relative (or "dualistic") context.

The question here is: Is it by way of this conventional, dualistic viewpoint that the verses of the Gospel of Thomas—reputed to have been uttered by Jesus—are intended to be understood? If not, what would be the alternative?

What do the *particular* things (any being, object, or condition), in our conceivable reality, comprise *in sum*? A whole; totality. For example, one particular thing is the star nearest to us, which we've named the "sun"; and such things that orbit around it, we have given other names —such as Venus, Earth, Mars, etc. Another of the named things, relative to this cosmology, is Earth's galaxy, which has been designated the Milky Way. Taken together, all such classes of things—and their entire constituent elements—are subsumed in the overarching totality that we call the "universe." The limited, relative entities—suns, planets, galaxies, etc.—are viewed by us as a subset of an all-inclusive cosmic wholeness which is unlimited by any of its comprising forms.

The very meaning we've attached to the word "universal" is that which "occurs everywhere," and as such is "all-inclusive."

The word *all* has itself historically been used as a prefix in referent phrases depicting "supreme being"—as indicative of "god"—such as the Almighty. The word *all* is nuanced to mean "any whatsoever," but also "more than," and additionally "lone" (or "sole").

It is this utmost, or ultimate, condition which is the focus of the awareness of the mystic whose sayings the Gospel of Thomas are the record. Jesus, here, is not speaking in the accustomed, dualistic terms of one who emphasizes the importance of the "many," but of one whose own consciousness is immersed in—and identified with—the "all." Throughout this Gospel, he makes it abundantly clear that his perspective is that of one who senses an immediate and direct interconnectedness with the supernal totality; and he invariably speaks of this with complete authority.

He views himself not merely as one of the "many" limited entities or forms which give the "all" its reality, but as that fully-encompassing reality itself in its wholeness. Unequivocally, he says; *"It is I who am the all."* (77) * Perceiving his own being as ultimately intrinsic with, and essential to, the universal totality, he adds: *"From me did the all* [every conceivable thing] *come forth, and unto me did the all extend* [in form]."†

He is clearly indicating that he knows this all as his own being, and that therefore not anything is absent from such an all-inclusive reality.

---

* A reminder that parenthetical numeration refers to the ordering of verses as found in the Thomas O. Lambdin translation.

† Bracketed constructions are mine.

"If one who knows the all still feels a personal deficiency," he remarks, *"he is completely deficient."* (67)

Thus, deficient is any person whose perception of reality is limited to an awareness of the "many," the relative aspects of the apparent universe, rather than recognizing the all-encompassing supercedence of the universal wholeness which knows of no insufficiency.

And the implication—since he is presumably speaking to interested disciples—is that not just he, Jesus, is the "I who am the all," but that everyone (any other "I") "who knows the all" will also no longer be personally deficient.

There is no doubt on the part of the addressed disciples, throughout the Gospel, that they clearly recognize that Jesus does indeed maintain a spiritual perspective which is different from their accustomed one. In fact, that is clearly the precise reason that they have been drawn to him as disciples. Like all such who have similarly quested, throughout world history, they desire to discover how the individuated "me" interrelates with the unlimited "all." They each seek to be for themselves—as with Jesus—"one who knows the all," in the same direct and immediate way that one knows oneself.

> *His disciples said to him, "Show us the place where you are, since it is necessary for us to seek it."* (24)

Jesus is evidently intimately familiar with the plight of the seeker and he has a reassuring attitude toward it, in more than one of his responses.

> *Seek and you will find.* (92)

> *Blessed are the hungry, for the belly of him who desires will be filled.* (69)

152

He compares what is to be found to a "pearl." He tells of

> ... *a merchant who had a consignment of merchandise and who discovered a pearl. That merchant was shrewd. He sold the merchandise and bought the pearl alone for himself.* (76)

And, similarly, he speaks of

> ... *a wise fisherman who cast his net into the sea and drew it up from the sea full of small fish. Among them the wise fisherman found a fine large fish. He threw all the small fish back into the sea and chose the large fish without difficulty.*

Lest this point concerning the "many" and the "one" go unnoticed, he then emphasized,

> *Whoever has ears to hear, let him hear.* (8)

Jesus, in this gospel, takes quite seriously the importance of the teachings he offers. He makes it clear that only one who clearly sees the way is in a position to point out the way:

> *Jesus said, 'If a blind man leads a blind man, they will both fall into a pit.'* (34)

And he assumes the responsibility for such guiding leadership; he says of Mary, in response to a criticism by Simon Peter,

> *I myself shall lead her...* (114)

Even more to the point that he has the rare authority to speak firsthand of the transcendent reality,

Jesus said, 'Many times have you desired to hear these words which I am saying to you, and you had no one else to hear them from.' (38)

He urged his listeners to seek the *"unfailing and enduring treasure"* (76):

Whoever finds himself is superior to the world. (111)

He holds out this promise:

Jesus said, 'He who will drink from my mouth will become like me [who am the all]. *I myself shall become he, and the things that are hidden will be revealed to him.'* (108)

Approvingly, Jesus says of Thomas: *"You have drunk…from the bubbling spring which I have measured out."* Because of which, Jesus then *"took him and withdrew and told him three things"*—privately, that were not revealed to Simon Peter and Matthew. (13)

Historically, such recondite teachings were not proffered to any who were not demonstrably sincere. Jesus' advice to those who, like him, had obtained this pearl:

Do not give what is holy to dogs, lest they throw them on the dung heap. Do not throw the pearls to swine. (93)

Notice the very first words of the prologue to the Gospel of Thomas: *"These are the secret sayings which the living Jesus spoke…"* And verse number one, which follows, attaches to these sayings a startling importance: *"Whoever finds the interpretation of these sayings will not experience death."* *

The opening notice, before any following sayings were given, is "find" for yourself "the interpretation" of what Jesus is presenting herein. To "interpret" *means* pointedly "to reveal the meaning of." It is clear that "the interpretation of these sayings" is meant to be uncovered by the perspicacious seeker.

> *Jesus said, "It is to those who are worthy of my mysteries that I tell my mysteries." (62)*

To those who are seriously dedicated to delving into the meaning of Jesus' sayings, he encourages:

> *He who seeks will find and ... will be let in. (94)*

Jesus tests three disciples for their aptitude (according to verse 13) regarding the understanding which each has of Jesus' perceived self-identity. Only the response of Thomas is acknowledged (more on the statement of Thomas later.†) Jesus indicates that both he and Thomas now share the same mastery concerning the interrelationship of the "me" to the "all," when he avows: *"I am not your master."*

He observes:

> *Because you have drunk, you have become intoxicated from the bubbling spring which I have measured out.*

As now worthy of his mysteries, Jesus gives Thomas an additional teaching.

---

* More on this later. See page 194.

† See page 167.

When Thomas returned to his companions, they asked him, "What did Jesus say to you?"

Thomas did not tell the two, who had previously failed to penetrate the significance of Jesus' arcane question.

To "measure out" the spiritual teachings is not the same as to obscure the teachings.

Jesus said, "Woe to the Pharisees, for they are like a dog sleeping in the manger of oxen, for neither does he eat nor does he let the oxen eat." (102)

Jesus makes clear that the intention of these sanctioned gatekeepers is to conceal the "unfailing and enduring treasure" from truth seekers.

The Pharisees and scribes have taken the keys of knowledge (gnosis) and hidden them. They themselves have not entered, nor have they allowed to enter those who wish to. (39)

Speaking of those in the world who were uninterested in the transcendent teachings in general, Jesus said,

… my soul became afflicted for the sons of men, because they are blind in their hearts and do not have sight… (28)

But if you will not know yourselves you dwell in poverty and it is you who are that poverty. (3)

That poverty, though, can be eradicated for those who persist to know themselves. Jesus describes

… a man who had a hidden treasure in his field without knowing it…. And the one who bought it went plowing and found the treasure. (109)

And he says:

When you come to know yourselves... you will realize that it is you who are the sons of the living father. (3)

In several instances, Jesus uses the words "living" and "live" to indicate a significant condition of presence, an essential category of being.

Jesus said, "Blessed is the man who has suffered and found life." (58)

Jesus said, "Take heed of the living one while you are alive, lest you die and seek to see him and be unable to do so." (59)

Jesus said, "Two will rest on a bed; the one will die, and the other will live." (61)

The one who lives from the living one will not see death.... Whoever finds himself is superior to the world. (111)

Plus, as the Gospel's opening sentence points out, these are the sayings "which the living Jesus spoke..."

When Simon Peter declared that one of the disciples, Mary, was "not worthy of life," Jesus said,

I myself shall lead her... so that she too may become a living spirit... (114)

What is being indicated concerning those who have *found* life and *become* the living, and the expression "When you come to know yourselves...you will realize"? To *realize* is "to make real; to bring into being; to understand fully." Realization has traditionally been a synonym for that mystical discovery by spiritual seekers which for millennia has been known as enlightenment. To "enlighten" is "to give the light of fact to: to free from ignorance; to make clear, reveal, or illuminate."

The teachings—when fully understood—will illuminate, reveal, the living condition of intimate knowledge of the all:

> Jesus said, 'He who will drink from my mouth will become like me... and the things that are hidden will be revealed to him.' (108)

"Show us," his disciples said to him, "the place where you are... for us to seek it." He said to them,

> Whoever has ears, let him hear. There is light within a man of light, and he lights up the whole world. If he does not shine, he is in darkness. (24)

> You, too, look for a place for yourself within repose, lest you become a corpse...(60)*

The word *place* for Jesus, in several verses, appears to have the meaning of "a situation, or state; a standing condition": Jesus said, "I took my place in the midst of the world... " (28)

This "place" or "state" of enlightenment that he says "he who seeks will find" would appear to be the subject of this parable, where the shepherd "looked for that one until he found it," in preference to the "many":

> Jesus said, "The kingdom is like a shepherd who had a hundred sheep. One of them, the largest, went astray. He left the ninety-nine and looked for that one until he found it. When he had gone to such trouble, he said to the sheep, 'I care for you more than the ninety-nine.'" (107)

As we proceed, a few of the words which are given as those of Jesus will clarify these passages, when their common usage in this Gospel is studied. For example, the word "kingdom" is frequently repeated, in a rather consistent context. In each case, the first thing that is noticeable

---

* Repose means "to be quiet and calm; peace of mind, or tranquility."

is that the kingdom in these references is relevant to a situation or circumstance that is attitudinal or experiential, in the same sense as a revelation would be.

> Jesus said, 'The kingdom is like a man who had a hidden treasure in his field without knowing it," ... [which a buyer then discovered.]

> The kingdom is like a shepherd [whose largest sheep was not seen: he] looked for that one until he found it.

> The kingdom of the father is like a merchant who had a consignment of merchandise and... sold the merchandise and bought the pearl... his unfailing and enduring treasure, where no moth comes near to devour and no worm destroys.

> The kingdom of the father is like a man who had good seed. (57)

In several passages, Jesus uses the word seed (or sowing) obviously to refer to the teachings, as a catalyst which begets "good fruit."

In a similar manner, fermenting yeast is used to connote a transformative influence:

> Jesus said, "The kingdom of the father is like a certain woman [who concealed] a little leaven... in some dough [resulting in] large loaves." (96)

And this kingdom also is associated with the serious intentions of the seeker.

> The kingdom of the father is like a certain man who, [in his own house, drew his sword and thrust it into a wall] in order to find out whether [he] could carry through. (98)

More to the point, this kingdom is one which a seeker is to enter in the here and now.

> *He said to them, "Those here who do the will of my father... will enter the kingdom..." (99)*

> *The Pharisees and the scribes... themselves have not entered, nor have they allowed to enter those who wish to.*

> *Yet I have said, whichever one of you comes to be a child* will be acquainted with the kingdom... (46)*

> *These infants... are like those who enter the kingdom....When you make... the above like the below... then you will enter... (22)†*

And

> *Jesus said, "I myself shall lead [Mary]... so that she too... will enter the kingdom..."*

It is the *teachings* which are germane to this kingdom:

The disciples said to Jesus, *"Tell us what the kingdom of heaven is like."* He said to them... *"It is the smallest of all seeds. But when it falls on tilled soil, it produces a great plant" (20)* ...if the seed takes root.

This is a kingdom in the sense of "a realm or domain," the "place" of enlightened realization and consequent "repose" (the experiential bliss of spiritual awareness), a condition which the benign enters and immerses oneself into. It is "the field" where its buyer "went plowing" by heeding the teachings, while declining to pursue distractions.

---

* Child: "without guile; benign, not corrupt"; also, "progeny with potential to mature."

† More on this verse, see section beginning page 191.

Jesus said, "Blessed are the solitary and elect, for you will find the kingdom." (49)

He who is near me is near the fire, and he who is far from me is far from the kingdom. (82)

If you do not fast as regards the world, you will not find the kingdom. (27)

This is a kingdom which is locatable here and now, because it is immanently present. His disciples said to him, *"When will the kingdom come?"*

It will not come by waiting for it. It will not be a matter of saying, "here it is" or "there it is." Rather, the kingdom of the father is spread out upon the earth, and men do not see it. (113)

If those who lead you say to you, "See, the kingdom is in the sky," then the birds of the sky will precede you. If they say to you, "It is in the sea," then the fish will precede you. Rather, the kingdom is inside of you, and it is outside of you. (3)

As regards the kingdom of this Gospel, there is no need "waiting for it"; any sincere one "who seeks will find."

"When you come to know yourselves, then... you will realize that it is you who are the sons of the living father," (because) *"the kingdom of the father is spread out upon the earth";* (however,) *"the sons of men... are blind in their hearts and do not have sight"* ...for the fire of illumination.

Jesus makes several references to "father," as well, in this gospel. This is, he tells us, a "living father" whose "kingdom" is not in "the sky" but "is spread out upon the earth."

This "kingdom of my father" would be the "place" that Jesus entered ("to go into; penetrate") to realize for himself what will be discovered "inside of you."

This is a father that they will "truly come to know"... "who have been persecuted within themselves" (69), having been troubled to look at the confusion within.

When Salome asks, *"Who are you..?",*

> *Jesus said to her, "I am he who exists from the undivided [All]. I was given some of the things of my father." (61)*

> *Jesus said, "A grapevine has been planted outside of the father, but being unsound, it will be pulled up by its roots and destroyed." (40)* *

This father is the source of gnosis, spiritual revelation, the predecessor in tradition that informs the child about the nature of life.

> *Blessed are those who have heard the word* [teachings] *of the father and have truly kept it. (79)*

> *It is the smallest of all seeds. But when it falls on tilled soil, it produces a great plant and becomes a shelter...*

Through self-realization, Jesus was given "the things" of the father, of the source of enlightened teachings.

Some disciples questioned, *"Who are you..?"* Jesus responded:

> *You do not realize who I am from what I say to you... (43)*

---

* A grapevine is profuse, branching, entangled, suggesting duality.

They said to him, 'Tell us who you are"... He said to them, "You read the face of the sky and of the earth, but you have not recognized the one* who is before you..." (91)

He said to them, "You have omitted the one living in your presence..." (52)

Yet, what you asked me about in former times and which I did not tell you then, now I do desire to tell, but you do not inquire after it. (92)

Recognize what is in your sight, and that which is hidden from you will become plain to you. (5)

Jesus said, "That which you have will save you if you bring it forth from yourselves." (70)

Because,

... the kingdom is inside of you, and it is outside of you†... come to know yourselves... and you will realize...

So, for those with sight—perception—the key, the gnosis, will be given whereby the all becomes clearly plain and evident, and *"that which you have will save you"* ("preserve from harm").

This is the "hidden" gnosis that Jesus *"did not tell you"* but now *"I do desire to tell,"* so that you will *"come to know yourselves"* and you *"will become like me"* (*"unto me did the all extend"*).

"Many times have you desired to hear these words"... and *"had no one else to hear them from,"* but now *"the things that are hidden will be revealed...."*

---

* Or, the "One".

† It is the All.

More than thirty specific verses (quotations attributed to Jesus) are given—bracketed between the first one and the last one—that cast light on the cryptic message, the gnosis that is disclosed in this gospel.

The allusions in the verses that follow (among about seventy that have not above been considered) reflect a pattern reminiscent of other, ancient teachings relevant to the perspective of that which is known as nonduality. They are sayings relating to a context of spiritual guidance that is universally and generally regarded as originating only with a person who has been recognized as having been "enlightened."

Common to these enlightenment teachings, at least as far back as written language, is a traditional term which is even more prominent and evocative than the descriptive word *all*.

The word *absolute* carries a meaning which comes closer to suggesting a designation, for the principal which is sought in nondual realization, than any other. The absolute is "completely unrestricted, not dependent upon anything else; not relative or limited." When capitalized, as it often is in spiritual passages, it is meant to indicate "ultimate reality, as eternal, infinite, omnipresent." It is characterized further as: "being, or presence, in its utmost condition, fundamental and essential to all that inclusively exists."

As the infinite, it is "unbounded, endless; ultimately beyond comprehension." And as the eternal, it "exists at all times; without beginning or end, enduring indefinitely, unceasingly permanent."

And it is inherently because of its infinite and eternal condition that it is singularly omnipresent. Omnipresent means: "in every possible location for any conceivable duration." Where this absolute actuality exists, a universal and perpetual phenomenon defines its mystical, enigmatic nature.

Entirely without any limitation or hindrance whatsoever, it is indivisibly present in its entire, unbroken totality at any and every point in space or time. Experiencing no restraints or boundaries whatsoever, it not only surrounds but permeates and saturates all that appears as being or existence itself. As such, it is the enveloping and penetrating essence of the extent of cosmic reality, everywhere, at any time.

From the standpoint of that which is acknowledged to be omnipresent, no separable categories as "here" or "there," as "now" or "then," pertain; all that is, was, or will be, material or immaterial, is inevitably informed by and conditional upon a wholeness or completeness that of itself transcends such disconnections or fragments as what are conceived of as parts or individuation.

For this reason, enlightenment scriptures emphasize that the true, basic, fundamental nature or characteristic that underlies the identity of all definable elements or aspects is inherently that of the ever-present Absolute. All "things" share a commonality or sameness, being subsumed in an interactive matrix that is categorically called "oneness."

This all-inclusive interconnectedness is what accommodates such paradoxical descriptions as the Absolute being at once "the beginning and the end" (sometimes called the "alpha and omega"), and other seemingly contradictory expressions.

This noumenon, or ground or field, is through which all phenomena take form; the unchanging and formless potentiality or plenum from which all changeable, impermanent forms appear and to which all ultimately recede. All of the relative "things," whatever object or entity, are therefore considered to be the perceivable manifestations of an all-encompassing Absolute.

This, evidently, was the understanding which permitted Jesus to articulate declarations that reflect those which characteristically only the exponents of nonduality have been reported to enunciate.

> *Jesus said.... "where the beginning is, there will the end be. Blessed is he who will take his place in the beginning; he will know the end ... "* (18)

> *His disciples said to him, "When will the kingdom come?" Jesus said ... "It will not be a matter of saying 'here it is' or 'there it is.'"* (113)

A significant aspect of the nondual epiphany is the realization that the formless source of the manifestations of entities or forms is not discernible itself as a separate, identifiable entity. Investing its being in all things that take existence, it has no particular, limited identity of its own. It can only inadequately be described by such conventional ambiguities as "both immanent and transcendent." By its illimitable, diffuse nature, it is incomprehensible—indeed inconceivable—to the pragmatic human mind.

For this reason, Jesus could only say, *"I am the all."*

When once *"Jesus said to his disciples... 'tell me who I am like,'"* Simon Peter failed the test by saying, *"You are like a righteous angel."* Likewise, Matthew failed: *"You are like a wise philosopher."* Thomas recognized that nothing can be said of that which is incomparable: *"Master, my mouth is wholly incapable of saying whom you are like."*

That is when Jesus approved Thomas' response:

> *I am not your master. Because you have drunk ... from the bubbling spring which I have measured out.* (13)

And Jesus then invested him with select teachings. This, too, is why,

> *Jesus said: "I shall give you what no eye has seen and what no ear has heard and what no hand has touched and what has never occurred to the human mind."* (17)

And why he could speak of an

> *...unfailing and enduring treasure where no moth comes near to devour and no worm destroys.* (76)

And he could point out:

> *"It will not come by waiting for it.... Rather, [it] is spread out upon the earth, and men do not see it."* (113)

Because the Absolute is at every point in the formed universe found—here or there, upper or lower, inner or outer—the Vedas have phrased it thus: *"nowhere is it not."* Any reality which the senses or mind can perceive is the Absolute in one of its many transient manifestations. As the Christian mystic Meister Eckhart affirmed, *"Who sees not God everywhere sees God nowhere."*

The profound realization of nondual enlightenment is that the very essence or core of the seeker itself is the omnipresent Absolute. As the scriptures and sutras have asserted, your "true nature," your fundamental identity, is that of the infinite and eternal Beingness. Again, the Vedas have stated in the most direct simplicity, *Tat Tvam Asi*: "That Thou Art." As Jesus put it, *"I am the all."* This gnosis is the true treasure to be unearthed in each lifetime.

> *Rather, the kingdom is inside of you, and it is outside of you. When you come to know yourselves, then you will become known, and you will realize that it is you...* (3)

> *Jesus said... "Do you not realize that he* [the "father"] *who made the inside is the same one who made the outside?"* (89)

> *Let him who seeks, continue seeking until he finds....and he will rule over the all.* (2)

> *You do not realize who I am...*

> *His disciples said to him, "Twenty-four prophets spoke in Israel, and all of them spoke in you." He said to them, "You have omitted the one living* * *in your presence... "* (52)

> *... you have not recognized the one who is before you, and you do not know how to read this moment.* (91)

> *His disciples said to him... "when will the new world come?" He said to them, "What you look forward to has already come, but you do not recognize it."* (51)

> *If one who knows the all still feels a personal deficiency, he is completely deficient.*

---

* Or, the living One?

It is the ubiquitous Absolute from which all of the apparent, relative images are manifest to the mind and senses—"the ten thousand things" (as Buddhism terms it)—that seemingly form the substance of our recognizable universe. These images (that we imagine to be "reality") are "a likeness or representation in form; an impression, or embodied conception."

These images, or appearances, each relate to the other and are dependent upon each other for their definition, for their identity. But the Absolute—self-originating, self-perpetuating—is "not dependent on anything else: perfect"; thus the ancient texts say that it is only this aspect which is actual and permanent, and all else changes in appearance, is impermanent and, by contrast, unreal.

It is not woman of which man is born, in this sense, but of the immediacy of the Absolute presence. This is why it has been said, "That you were, before you were born." If it were otherwise, the relative "you" would not have appeared, you would not exist. The point of this recognition is that the relative "you" has never, in any way, been apart from, separate from, the all-pervasive Absolute.

When the seeker has penetrated to this self-realization, she disappears as a unique individual, into the anonymity of the Totality (the All) itself. This, then, is heaven: a place of harmony, tranquility, and repose; the bliss of inner peace to which the Upanishads have alluded. The perceived individuated self is now aware of its inseparable transcendency as the intrinsic essence, the Self (as the venerable scriptures capitalize it to represent the Absolute).

Jesus said… "that which is hidden from you will become plain to you ["what is in your sight"]. For there is nothing hidden which will not become manifest." (5)

And,

…for all things are plain in the sight of heaven. For nothing hidden will not become manifest, and nothing covered will remain without being uncovered. (6)

Also,

Jesus said, "Blessed are the solitary and elect, for you will find the kingdom. For you are from it, and to it you will return." (49)

[The father] will become manifest, but his image will remain concealed by his light. ….The images are manifest to man, but the light in them remains concealed in the image of the light of the father. (83)

Jesus said, "When you see your likeness, you rejoice. But when you see your images which came into being before you, and which neither die nor become manifest, how much you will have to bear!" (84)

Jesus said, "If they say to you, 'Where did you come from?', say to them, "We came from the light, the place where the light came into being on its own accord and established (itself) and became manifest through their image." If they say to you, "Is it you?", say, "We are its children, and we are the elect of the living father." If they ask you, "What is the sign of your father in you?", say to them, "It is movement and repose." (50)

Jesus said, "Blessed is he who came into being before he came into being. If you become my disciples and listen to my words, these stones will minister to you." (19)

For there will be days when you will say, "Blessed are the womb which has not conceived…" (79)

170

Stillness / being / presence is the teacher (eg. stones/nature etc.)

presence in everything!

Jesus said, "When you see one who was not born of woman, prostrate yourselves on your faces and worship him. That one is your father." (15)

Jesus said, "I took my place in the midst of the world, and I* appeared to them in flesh." (28)

The Absolute, being itself unrestricted by identification as a relative, or limited, entity, it has sometimes been referred to as "nothingness" ("not any particular thing; indistinguishable"), or "emptiness," or as the "void." In abdicating one's sense of personal, separate identity, in the advent of nondual enlightenment, one sheds the ego-centric or "self"-centered perspective that is the primary characteristic of our social conditioning and enculturation.

This has sometimes been poetically described as "ego death," the ceasing of a sense of a bounded "I-ness": to discern that one's true, ultimate identity is as that of nothingness itself. All beings are, ultimately, imbued with the same mutual, consistent, indivisible and essential beingness. The "you" and "me" distinctions are seen to be superficial or illusory.

Jesus said, "Two will rest on a bed: the one will die, and the other will live.... Therefore I say, if he is destroyed he will be filled with light, but if he is divided, he will be filled with darkness." (61)

And,

... empty they came into the world, and empty too they seek to leave the world. (28)

---

* Try replacing 'I', with 'the Self'.

He said, "O lord, there are many around the drinking trough, but there is nothing in the cistern." (74)

You, however, be as wise as serpents and as innocent as doves. (39)

To shed the false ego is as to disrobe or undress, to lay bare one's natural being. And the field, or Absolute, is one that no one can exclusively possess, such as "my kingdom" or "your kingdom."

Mary said to Jesus: *"Whom are your disciples like?"*

They are like children who have settled in a field which is not theirs. When the owners of the field come, they will say, "Let us have back our field." They (will) undress in their presence in order to let them have back their field and to give it back to them." (21)

His disciples said, "When will you become revealed to us and when shall we see you?" Jesus said, "When you disrobe without being ashamed and take up your garments and place them under your feet like little children and tread on them, then (will you see) the son of the living one, and you will not be afraid." (37)

Jesus said, "The angels and prophets will come to you and give to you those things you (already) have. And you too, give them those things which you have, and say to yourselves, 'When will they come and take what is theirs?'" (88)

An instructive parable, that is unique to this Gospel, is cited, concerning the way a person makes it "home": Jesus said,

The kingdom of the (father) is like a certain woman who was carrying a (jar) full of meal. While she was walking (on the) road, still some distance from home, the handle of the jar broke and the meal emptied out behind her (on) the road. She did not realize it: she had noticed no accident. When she reached her house, she set the jar down and found it empty. (97)

172

The jar is her self; the meal is her ego, or "self"-consciousness. On the path—with "getting home" her intention—she finally is devoid of her ego, without sensing that as a loss. Hers was an emptied jar, in arriving home—a changed awareness, no longer that of a seeker or burden-carrier.

◎

There is a significant, indicative phrasing which is a hallmark of enlightenment, or nondual, teachings. The Absolute is a peerless singularity; it occupies, and is present as, anything which exists as animate or inanimate, substantial or insubstantial, tangible or intangible. Descriptive in the ancient texts are words such as "no division" and "One, without a second." In fact, the Sanskrit term for the point of view of nonduality is *Advaita*, which has the literal meaning of "not two."

There are nearly twenty sayings in this Gospel which, in one manner or another, provide commentary on dualistic divisiveness, the central concern of Advaita:

> Jesus said, "A grapevine has been planted outside of the father, but being unsound, it will be pulled up by its roots and destroyed." (40)

> Jesus said, "It is impossible for a man to mount two horses or to stretch two bows. And it is impossible for a servant to serve two masters; otherwise, he will honor the one and treat the other contemptuously." (47)

> His disciples said to him, "When will the kingdom come?" The reply: "It will not come by waiting for it. It will not be a matter of saying, 'here it is' or 'there it is.'" (113)

Jesus said, "The kingdom is like a shepherd who had a hundred sheep. One of them, the largest, went astray. He left the ninety-nine and looked for that one [One] until he found it. When he had gone to such trouble, he said to the sheep, 'I care for you more than the ninety-nine.'" (107)

Jesus said, "He who will drink from my mouth will become like me. I myself shall become he, and the things that are hidden will be revealed to him." (108)

Salome said, "Who are you..?" Jesus said to her, "I am he who exists from the undivided." (61)

A man said to him, "Tell my brothers to divide my father's possessions with me." He said to him, "O man, who has made me a divider?" He turned to his disciples and said to them, "I am not a divider, am I?" (72)

Upon birth we transit, from the coherent unity of repose in the Absolute, into the ever-changing movement of the world of duality— to again seek to dwell in that repose.

When you come to dwell in the light, what will you do? On the day when you were one you became two. But when you become two, what will you do? (11)

Jesus said, "Many are standing at the door, but it is the solitary who will enter the bridal chamber." (75)

Jesus said, "I shall choose you, one out of a thousand, and two out of ten thousand, and they shall stand as a single one." (23)

"Therefore I say, if he is destroyed he will be filled with light, but if he is divided, he will be filled with darkness." (61)

Jesus said, "When you make the two one, you will become the sons of man, and when you say, 'Mountain, move away,' it will move away." (106)

(Jesus said ...), *"I am afraid that you will go intending to pull up the weeds and pull up the wheat along with them."* (57)

Jesus said, "If two make peace with each other in this one house, they will say to the mountain, 'Move away,' and it will move away." (48)

Jesus said, "Wretched is the body that is dependent upon a body, and wretched is the soul that is dependent on these two." (87)

Jesus said, "The man old in days will not hesitate to ask a small child seven days old about the place of life, and he will live. For many who are first will become last, and they will become one and the same." (4)

Jesus saw infants being suckled. He said to his disciples, "These infants being suckled are like those who enter the kingdom." They said to him, "Shall we then, as children, enter the kingdom?" Jesus said to them, "When you make the two one, and when you make the inside like the outside and the outside like the inside, and the above like the below, and when you make the male and the female one and the same, so that the male not be male and the female female ... then will you enter the kingdom." (22)

Simon Peter said to them, "Let Mary leave us, for women are not worthy of life." Jesus said, "I myself shall lead her in order to make her male, so that she too may become a living spirit resembling you males. For every woman who will make herself male will enter the kingdom of heaven." (114)

Jesus' realization was apparently that, indivisibly, all things are superimposed on the One, and the One is the substrate of all things: "this" and "that," "here" and "there," the manyness and the oneness are inseparably and simultaneously one and the same actuality. Jesus was aware that, as the self/Self, this presence was not apart or disconnected from any element or aspect, at any time or place. The following does not appear in the canonical gospels, and would have been spoken by an enlightened teacher of nonduality:

Jesus said, "It is I who am the light which is above them all. It is I who am the all. From me did the all come forth, and unto me did the all extend. Split a piece of wood, and I am there. Lift up the stone, and you will find me there." (77)

◎

Eradicating the erroneous supposition of the reality of the "you/me" or "this/that" dichotomy is to transcend the polarizing disparities innate in our dualistic conditioning. More than fifteen of the Gospel's attributions to Jesus are germane to the matter of the presence which remains once the ego, or "I" focus, has been unhoused and the construct known as the differentiating *"person*ality*"* has become dismantled. Enduring then is the nondual clarity described as Self-knowledge, or insightful illumination.

His disciples said to him, "Who are you, that you should say these things to us?" (43)

His disciples said to him, "Show us the place where you are… "

They said to him, "Tell us who you are so that we may believe [in] *you."* (91)

Salome said, "Who are you, man..?"

Jesus said to his disciples, "Compare me to someone and tell me whom I am like.." Simon Peter said to him, "You are like a righteous angel." Matthew said to him, "You are like a wise philosopher." (13)

Jesus said, "It is I who am the light which is above them all." (77)

He said to them, "Whoever has ears, let him hear. There is light within a man of light, and he lights up the whole world. If he does not shine, he is darkness." (24)

There will be days when you will look for me and will not find me. (38)

I myself shall become he… (108)

… become a living spirit… who… will enter the kingdom of heaven. (114)

When you come to know yourselves, then you will become known, and you will realize that it is you who are the sons of the living father. But if you will not know yourselves you dwell in poverty and it is you who are that poverty. (3)

His disciples said, "When will you become revealed to us and when shall we see you?" Jesus said, "When you disrobe… then you will see the son of the living one, and you will not be afraid." (37)

He said to them, "You have omitted the one living in your presence…" (52)

Jesus said, "Adam came into being from a great power and a great wealth…" (85)

Indeed, I am amazed at how this great wealth has made its home in this poverty*. (29).

… woe to the soul that depends on the flesh. (112)

The message is to empty the unreliable jar, to strip off your inculcated dualistic conditioning without fear.

Therefore I say, if he is destroyed he will be filled with light, but if he is divided, he will be filled with darkness. (61)

Jesus said, "I shall destroy this house, and no one will be able to build it [again]." (71)†

He who is near me is near the fire… (82)

---

* Suggesting the poverty of the "you" in the world which does not know itself.

† Suggesting that once self-identity is completely vacated, it does not recur.

For Jesus, there is a prime concern, in this Gospel, referenced in more than twenty verses. The teachings are to be, first, clearly heard and thoroughly comprehended, then they must be faithfully acted upon— *lived.* The hearers are surely to be an influence upon others, as the difference in their behavior is noticed. The crux is that, in living your life as an awakened one, you are a vital expression of the truth to be found in the unitive teachings. This is the infectious, non-verbal transmission of the dharma, which is at least as instructive as spoken teachings might be.

> *Jesus said, "Grapes are not harvested from thorns, nor are figs gathered from thistles, for they do not produce fruit. A good man brings forth good from his storehouse... "* (45)

> *Blessed are those who have heard the word of the father and have truly kept it.* (79)

> *Those here who do... are my brothers... who will enter the kingdom of my father.* (99)

Now is the time to awaken:

> *Jesus said, "There was a rich man who had much money. He said, 'I shall put my money to use so that I may sow, reap, plant, and fill my storehouse with produce, with the result that I shall lack nothing.' Such were his intentions, but that same night he died. Let him who has ears hear."* (63)

> *Jesus said, "Take heed of the living one [One] while you are alive, lest you die and seek to see him and be unable to do so."* (59)

> *Jesus said, "Blessed are they who have been persecuted within themselves. It is they who have truly come to know the father."* (69)

Jesus said, "I took my place in the midst of the world, and I appeared to them in flesh.... I found none of them thirsty.... When they shake off their wine, then they will repent." (28)

He was cognizant that some—even the closest to him—would fail to appreciate the wealth of the teachings.

[A] son did not know about the treasure. He inherited [his father's] field and sold it. (109)

Do not give what is holy to dogs.... Do not throw the pearls to swine, lest they [trample it underfoot]. (93)

These listeners, who were mistakenly expecting to be led somewhere into the distant future, he referred to a brother (likewise born of the Absolute).

The disciples said to Jesus, "We know that you will depart from us. Who is to be our leader?" Jesus said to them, "Wherever you are, you are to go to James the righteous, for whose sake heaven and earth came into being." (12)

Those in "darkness" and "unthirsty" for the life-giving way might even be one's parents or siblings.

Jesus said, "Whoever does not hate his father and his mother cannot become a disciple to me. And whoever does not hate his brothers and sisters and take up his cross in my way will not be worthy of me." (55)*

There would (like Thomas) be the rare adherent who became awakened and "filled with light"; Jesus anticipated that such would, like himself, propagate the spiritual teachings with acquired clarity:

---

* The verb *hate*, here, is likely intended in the sense of "to dislike, disgust to the point of discomfort or aversion"; e.g., "I hate selfishness."

For *"the one who lives from the living one"* the *"heavens and earth will be rolled up* [into one] *in your presence."* (111)

> When you cast the beam out of your own eye, then you will see clearly to cast the mote from your brother's eye. (26)

> Jesus said, *"Love your brother like your soul, guard him like the pupil of your eye."* (25)

> And the one who...found the treasure...began to lend money at interest to whomever he wished. (109)

> ...the true circumcision in spirit [removing the expendable] has become completely profitable. (53)

> Jesus said, *"Preach from your housetops that which you will hear in your ear. For no one lights a lamp and puts it under a bushel, nor does he put it in a hidden place, but rather he sets it on a lampstand so that everyone who enters and leaves will see its light."* (33)

> Jesus said, *"A city being built on a high mountain and fortified cannot fall, nor can it be hidden."* (32)

> Jesus said, *"The harvest is great but the laborers are few. Beseech the lord, therefore, to send out laborers to the harvest."* (73)

> Jesus said, *"Now the sower went out, took a handful (of seeds), and scattered them. Some fell on the road; the birds came and gathered them up. Others fell on rock, did not take root in the soil, and did not produce ears. And others fell on thorns; they choked the seed(s) and worms ate them. And others fell on the good soil and it produced good fruit: it bore sixty per measure and a hundred and twenty per measure."* (9)

Let there be among you a man of understanding. When the grain ripened, he came quickly with his sickle in his hand and reaped it. Whoever has ears to hear let him hear. (21)

Jesus cautioned, from his own experience, that not everyone will be found to be receptive to the message, or even the messenger. In a parable (65), "a good man who owned a vineyard" sent three messengers to the tenant farmers who leased it; the messengers did not return with any resultant produce.

In an even longer parable, a master sent a servant to invite guests to his meal: all four were too busy, with worldly affairs, to be present.

The master said to his servant, "Go outside to the streets and bring back those whom you happen to meet, so that they may dine." Businessmen and merchants (will) not enter the places of my father. (64)

Some will disdain the teachings, others may disdain the teacher: they

have become like [those who] ... *love the tree and hate its fruit, or love the fruit and hate the tree.* (43)

Among the more difficult aspects of the nondual, or enlightenment, teachings to communicate is the issue implicit concerning the immutable immediacy of the Presence. Because the self and the Self are already (have been, and always will be) one and the same actuality, one need not lift a finger nor move one inch to affect a unification with absolute Presence. This liberating insight is the essence of the nondual realization that ends the seeker's pursuit; as is pointed out in the ancient texts, "The seeker *is* the sought."

Since the seeker has inevitably come to know the Absolute in perceiving his own innate identity, no amount of finite time is involved in bringing omnipresent Being into the immediate moment: at no time, and in no place, has it not already been existent. Further, being itself perfect ("wholly complete, without omission; unsurpassingly excellent"), that which is a manifest embodiment of the Absolute—in whatever form or event—is incontrovertibly without inherent inadequacy, exactly as it is.

In consequence, the object of enlightened awareness is not expressed in an incessant drive for improvement of the transitory "self." The point of enlightenment can be understood as thorough resolution of conflict, inner and outer, and clarity of perception which results in relaxed repose. Complete intuitive awakening is the emphasis, rather than merely modifying one's inculcated state of confusion.

And considering that the Absolute is the essence of all that is, it therefore is the sustaining condition of the developments which unfold as "positive" or "negative," "good" or "bad" (by the limited human viewpoint). To the Self-realized, all things which occur or appear *are* as they *ought* to be (grandly obviating mankind's requisite approval or rejection).

Also, everything that is relative, limited, and impermanent is changeable, arising as an expression of the Absolute and eventually resolving into its immensity again. So in the words of the sages, "*That* is the do-er of what is done." This is understood to indicate that whether a person does—or does not do—good deeds, it is invariably the action of the Absolute in every case.

For this reason, there are no recommended practices or disciplines that can bring closer the Presence which one already exists as. To follow a ritualistic practice is to presume that some attainment is to be achieved at some eventual time, rather than recognizing *"That* thou *art"* here and now.

Even the solitude, quiet, and contemplation that are generally involved in reducing the distractions that obscure inner insight are not to be considered a means to an end but a milieu in which the psyche effortlessly empties of striving and ambition without that even being a goal.

So, the teachings indicate that one need not follow doctrinal or enculturated codes of behavior in order to be spiritually whole, or holy. Zealous meditation, pious fasting, beseeching prayer are viewed as missing the mark.

In this Gospel, Jesus reminds seekers, "It will not come by waiting for it." He said to them, "What you look forward to has already come, but you do not recognize it."

One need not "believe" in what is already clearly present.

> They said to him, "Tell us who you are so that we may believe in you." He said to them, "You read the face of the sky and of the earth, but you have not recognized the one who is before you, and you do not know how to read this moment." (91)
>
> Jesus said, "Why do you wash the outside of the cup? Do you not realize that he who made the inside is the same one who made the outside?" (89)
>
> Jesus said, "Come unto me, for my yoke is easy and my lordship is mild, and you will find repose for yourselves." (90)
>
> Jesus said, "If those who lead you say to you, 'See, the kingdom is in the sky,' then the birds of the sky will precede you. If they say to you, 'It is in the sea,' then the fish will precede you."

Misguiding "leaders" are the thorny vines from which grapes are not harvested, the thorns that choked the seeds "and worms ate them."

> (They saw) a Samaritan carrying a lamb on his way to Judea. He said to his disciples, "That man is round about the lamb." They said to him, "So that he may kill and eat it." He said to them, "While it is alive, he will not eat it, but only when he has killed it and it has become a corpse." They said to him, "He cannot do so otherwise." He said to them, "You too, look for a place for yourselves within repose, lest you become a corpse and be eaten." (60)

> And new wine is not put into old wineskins, lest they burst; nor is old wine put into a new wineskin, lest it spoil it. An old patch is not sewn into a new garment, because a tear would result. (47)

Jesus also, conspicuously, does not affirm religiosity, aimed as it is toward an accumulative gain.

> His disciples questioned him and said to him, "Do you want us to fast? How shall we pray? Shall we give alms? What diet shall we observe?" Jesus said, "Do not tell lies, and do not do what you hate, for all things are plain in the sight of heaven." (6)

Those who have consummated the unitive wedding, who regard each self as the Absolute, will not be found in default nor view themselves as deficient. Before all else, though, you need to clarify, "Who am I?"

> They said to Jesus, "Come, let us pray today and let us fast." Jesus said, "What is the sin that I have committed, or wherein have I been defeated? But when the bridegroom leaves the bridal chamber, then let them fast and pray." (104)

The Sabbath (Hebrew: "to rest"), emphasized by Jesus, is dedicated to repose and withdrawal from ambition and acquisitiveness, a "fast as regards the world."

If you do not fast as regards the world, you will not find the kingdom. If you do not observe the Sabbath as a Sabbath, you will not see the father. (27)

Jesus, in this Gospel, did not condone the religious practice of dietary restrictions, nor the ritual of circumcision.

Jesus said to them, "If you fast, you will give rise to sin for yourselves; and if you pray, you will be condemned; and if you give alms, you will do harm to your spirits. When you go into any land and walk about in the districts, if they receive you, eat what they will set before you, and heal the sick among them. For what goes into your mouth will not defile you, but that which issues from your mouth —it is that which will defile you." (14)

His disciples said to him, "Is circumcision beneficial or not?" He said to them, "If it were beneficial, their father would beget them already circumcised from their mother. Rather, the true circumcision in spirit has become completely profitable." (53)

Of the (fewer than thirty) verses yet to be referenced, a majority reveal the teacher's directives regarding one's awakened life in the relative, mundane world. What is "completely profitable" is to abstain from material achievement and acquisitiveness, self-serving temporal pursuits, and distractions from the "spirit" in general.

Jesus said ... it is impossible for a servant to serve two masters ...

Jesus said, "The kingdom of the father is like a merchant who had a consignment of merchandise and who discovered a pearl. That merchant was shrewd. He sold the merchandise and bought the pearl alone for himself. You too, seek his unfailing and enduring treasure where no moth comes near to devour and no worm destroys." (76)

Jesus said, "There was a rich man who had much money. He said, 'I shall put my money to use so that I may sow, reap, plant, and fill my storehouse with produce, with the result that I shall lack nothing.' Such were his intentions, but that same night he died. Let him who has ears hear." (63)

Of the four invited guests who, due to financial and social activities, did "not have spare time" to partake of a master's offerings (verse 64), Jesus concludes: *"Businessmen and merchants will not enter the places of my father."*

Jesus said, "I have cast fire upon the world, and see, I am guarding it until it blazes." (10)

Jesus said … "Whoever finds himself is superior to the world." (111)

Jesus said, "Whoever finds the world and becomes rich, let him renounce the world." (110)

Jesus said, "Whoever has come to understand the world has found (only) a corpse, and whoever has found a corpse is superior to the world." (56)

Jesus said, "He who has recognized the world has found the body, but he who has found the body is superior to the world." (80)

Jesus said, "Woe to the flesh that depends on the soul; woe to the soul that depends on the flesh." (112)

Jesus said, "Now the sower went out, took a handful (of seeds), and scattered them. Some fell on the road; the birds came and gathered them up. Others fell on rock, did not take root in the soil, and did not produce ears.'" (9)

Therefore I say, if the owner of a house knows that the thief is coming, he will begin his vigil before he comes and will not let him dig through into his house of his domain to carry away his goods. You, then, be on your guard against the world. Arm yourselves with great strength lest the robbers find a way to come to you, for the difficulty which you expect will (surely) materialize. Let there be among you a man of understanding. When the grain ripened, he came quickly with his sickle in his hand and reaped it. Whoever has ears to hear let him hear." (21)

Jesus said, "It is not possible for anyone to enter the house of a strong man and take it by force unless he binds his hands; then he will (be able to) ransack his house." (35)

Jesus said, "Fortunate is the man who knows where the brigands will enter, so that (he) may get up, muster his domain, and arm himself before they invade." (103)

The one who *"began to lend money at interest to whomever he pleased"* (verse 109) was spreading the wealth of the immaterial "hidden treasure" that he had found. Therefore, Jesus is not contradicting himself when he says of material wealth,

If you have money do not lend it at interest, but give (it) to one from whom you will not get it back. (95)

Jesus said, "Blessed are the poor, for yours is the kingdom of heaven." (54)

They showed Jesus a gold coin and said to him, "Caesar's men demand taxes from us." He said to them, "Give Caesar what belongs to Caesar, give God what belongs to God, and give me what is mine." (100)

And he said, "The man is like a wise fisherman who cast his net into the sea and drew it up from the sea full of small fish. Among them the wise fisherman found a fine large fish. He threw all the small fish back into the sea and chose the large fish without difficulty. Whoever has ears to hear, let him hear." (8)

Jesus said, "The kingdom is like a shepherd who had a hundred sheep. One of them, the largest, went astray. He left the ninety-nine and looked for that one until he found it. When he had gone to such trouble, he said to the sheep, 'I care for you more than the ninety-nine.'" (107)

Jesus said, "Do not be concerned from morning until evening and from evening until morning about what you will wear." (36)

Jesus said, "Let him who has grown rich be king, and let him who possesses power renounce it." (81)

... But if you will not know yourselves you dwell in poverty and it is you who are that poverty. (3)

And, simply, in two words:

Become passers-by. (42)

The enlightened person is alone ("all one"), now singular, at one with the eminence, no longer a "follower," and—recognizing the Absolute even as one's own essence or soul—having no need to be a "believer." To fully live from the self-less gnosis is to subsist on the edge of material insecurity. Additionally, one's perspective on earthly values will likely not be shared by even those closest.

Jesus said, "Blessed are they who have been persecuted within themselves. It is they who have truly come to know the father." (69)

Jesus said, "Let him who seeks continue seeking until he finds. When he finds, he will become troubled. When he becomes troubled, he will be astonished, and he will rule over the all." (2)

But "the difficulty which you expect will surely materialize."

Jesus said, "No prophet is accepted in his own village; no physician heals those who know him." (31)

Jesus said, "Show me the stone which the builders have rejected. That one is the cornerstone." (66)

Jesus said, "He who knows the father and the mother will be called the son of a harlot." (105)

Jesus said, "He who is near me is near the fire, and he who is far from me is far from the kingdom." (82)

Jesus said, "Woe to the pharisees, for they are like a dog sleeping in the manger of oxen, for neither does he eat nor does he (let) the oxen eat." (102)

And he took him and withdrew and told him three things. When Thomas returned to his companions, they asked him, "What did Jesus say to you?" Thomas said to them, "If I tell you one of the things which he told me, you will pick up stones and throw them at me; a fire will come out of the stones and burn you up." (13)

Jesus said, "Blessed is the man who has suffered and found life." (58)

... Then the owner sent his son and said, "Perhaps they will show respect to my son." Because the tenants knew that it was he who was the heir to the vineyard, they seized him and killed him. Let him who has ears hear. (65)

Jesus said, "Blessed are you when you are hated and persecuted. Wherever you have been persecuted they will find no place." (68)

Jesus said, "(The foxes have their holes) and the birds have their nests, but the son of man has no place to lay his head and rest." (86)

A woman from the crowd said to him, "Blessed are the womb which bore you and the breasts which nourished you." He said to (her),

Blessed are those who have heard the word of the father and have truly kept it. For there will be days when you will say, "Blessed are the womb which has not conceived and the breasts which have not given milk." (79)

The disciples said to him, "Your brothers and your mother are standing outside." He said to them, "Those who do the will of my father are my brothers and my mother. It is they who will enter the kingdom of my father." (99)

Jesus said, "Whoever does not hate his father and his mother cannot become a disciple to me. And whoever does not hate his brothers and sisters and take up his cross in my way will not be worthy of me." (55)

Jesus said, "Whoever blasphemes against the father will be forgiven, and whoever blasphemes against the son will be forgiven, but whoever blasphemes against the holy spirit will not be forgiven either on earth or in heaven." (44)

Whoever does not hate his (father) and his mother as I do cannot become a (disciple) to me. And whoever does (not) love his (father and) his mother as I do cannot become a (disciple to) me. For my mother [gave me birth] * but (my) true (mother) gave me life. (101)

Jesus said, "Men think, perhaps, that it is peace which I have come to cast upon the world. They do not know that it is dissension which I have come to cast upon the earth: fire, sword, and war. For there will be five in a house: three will be against two, and two against three, the father against the son, and the son against the father. And they will stand solitary." (16)

Jesus said, "Blessed are the solitary and elect, for you will find the kingdom. For you are from it, and to it you will return." (49)

Jesus said, "I shall choose you, one out of a thousand, and two out of ten thousand, and they shall stand as a single one." (23)

Jesus said, "Many are standing at the door, but it is the solitary who will enter the bridal chamber." (75)

---

* My extrapolation.

Due to the varied contexts of their metaphorical usages, the enlightenment scriptures concerning "birth" and "death," or beginning and ending, can be among the more difficult to apprehend.

The eternal Absolute, by its nature, is regarded as "unborn and undying"; it is, at the same time, indicated to be "the beginning and the end," Alpha and Omega, as the overarching infinity in which the finite and impermanent takes form.

Hence, realizing the essence of *all* things as the Absolute, a sage might say from that perception, *"I was not born to life, thus I will not die to life."*

He might proceed to say of his spiritual awakening, "I was born into the fullness of life."

A newborn infant is similar to a person who has sunk into a deep, dreamless sleep—empty of conceptual ideation and relative, dualistic mentation—where even the sense of assuming a particular identity is absent. In this condition, even the notional thoughts of "birth" and "death," or beginnings and endings, are absent. Thus, a sage might also say, "Birth and death are concepts, ideas."

Jesus, in this Gospel, speaks of coming "to be a child," and also of removing the "fine garments" of egoism which hide "the truth"; to become "innocent as doves."

> Jesus saw infants being suckled. He said to his disciples, "These infants being suckled are like those who enter the kingdom." (22)

> Jesus said, "Among those born of women, from Adam until John the Baptist, there is no one so superior to John the Baptist that his eyes should not be lowered (before him). Yet I have said, whichever one of you comes to be a child will be acquainted with the kingdom and will become superior to John." (46)

Jesus said, "Why have you come out into the desert? To see a reed shaken by the wind? And to see a man clothed in fine garments (like your) kings and your great men? Upon them are the fine garments, and they are unable to discern the truth." (78)

His disciples said, "When will you become revealed to us and when shall we see you?" Jesus said, "When you disrobe without being ashamed and take up your garments and place them under your feet like little children and tread on them, then (will you see) the son of the living one, and you will not be afraid." (37)

Jesus said, "Do not be concerned from morning until evening and from evening until morning about what you will wear." (36)

Mary said to Jesus, "Whom are your disciples like?" He said, "They are like children who have settled in a field which is not theirs. When the owners of the field come, they will say, 'Let us have back our field.' They (will) undress in their presence in order to let them have back their field and to give it back to them." (21)

Alternately, he speaks of a supernal condition; a "womb which has not conceived," a man "not born of woman."

Jesus said, "When you see one who was not born of woman, prostrate yourselves on your faces and worship him. That one is your father." (15)

Whoever does not hate his father and his mother as I do cannot become a disciple to me. And whoever does not love his father and his mother as I do cannot become a disciple to me. For my mother (...), but my true mother gave me life. (101)

Jesus said, "If they say to you, 'Where did you come from?', say to them, 'We came from the light, the place where the light came into being on its own accord and established (itself) and became manifest through their image.' If they say to you, 'Is it you?', say, 'We are its children, and we are the elect of the living father.' If they ask you, 'What is the sign of your father in you?', say to them, 'It is movement and repose.'" (50)

The dead are not alive, and the living will not die…. When you come to dwell in the light, what will you do? On the day when you were one you became two. But when you become two, what will you do? (11)

Jesus said, "I took my place in the midst of the world, and I appeared to them in flesh. I found all of them intoxicated; I found none of them thirsty. And my soul became afflicted for the sons of men, because they are blind in their hearts and do not have sight; for empty they came into the world, and empty too they seek to leave the world. But for the moment they are intoxicated. When they shake off their wine, then they will repent." (28)

The disciples said to Jesus, "Tell us how our end will be." Jesus said, "Have you discovered, then, the beginning, that you look for the end? For where the beginning is, there will the end be. Blessed is he who will take his place in the beginning; he will know the end and will not experience death." (18)

Jesus said, "Blessed is he who came into being before he came into being. If you become my disciples and listen to my words, these stones will minister to you." (19)

Jesus said, "Blessed are the solitary and elect, for you will find the kingdom. For you are from it, and to it you will return." (49)

As with birth, much of what the scriptures say specifically about death appears, on the surface, to be paradoxical. For instance, the unawakened are "dead": and although an awakened one is now fully "in life," she is "dead to this world." Furthermore, "ego-death" (which is occasionally spoken of) is viewed as the realization of the non-existence of the "individual" self, in which one has "died while alive."

Again, one who realizes the eternal ("timeless, without duration; changeless") and infinite as the permanent actuality from which arises one's own being, that being will be understood to subside into absolute Being, without ever having been separately apart from it: the venerable analogy has been the appearance and disappearance of an ocean wave.

Jesus, in this Gospel, intimates that those "living" in the "light" have recognized that the undivided, omnipresent essence is always already where it will everlastingly be: we have not been and will not be apart from the essential Presence, which has always been *here now*—no matter where "here" is or when "now" is.

The phrase *"will not experience death"* appears in the very first verse; it is repeated in verse 19, and supported across the textual passages.

> Jesus said, "Adam came into being from a great power and a great wealth, but he did not become worthy of you. For had he been worthy, (he would) not (have experienced) death." (85)

> The disciples said to Jesus, "Tell us how our end will be." Jesus said, "Have you discovered, then, the beginning, that you look for the end? For where the beginning is, there will the end be. Blessed is he who will take his place in the beginning; he will know the end and will not experience death." (18)

> Jesus said, "This heaven will pass away, and the one above it will pass away. The dead are not alive, and the living will not die. In the days when you consumed what is dead, you made it what is alive. When you come to dwell in the light, what will you do? On the day when you were one you became two. But when you become two, what will you do?" (11)

> Jesus said, "Blessed is the lion which becomes man when consumed by man; and cursed is the man whom the lion consumes, and the lion becomes man." (7)

Jesus said, "The heavens and the earth will be rolled up in your presence. And the one who lives from the living one will not see death." Does not Jesus say, "Whoever finds himself is superior to the world?" (111)

A long colloquy follows:

Jesus said, "Two will rest on a bed: the one will die, and the other will live."
Salome said, "Who are you, man, that you ... have come up on my couch and eaten from my table?"
Jesus said to her, "I am he who exists from the undivided. I was given some of the things of my father."
(...) I am your disciple.
(...) Therefore I say, if he is destroyed he will be filled with light, but if he is divided, he will be filled with darkness. (61)

Jesus said, "That which you have will save you if you bring it forth from yourselves. That which you do not have within you (will) kill you if you do not have it within you." (70)

Jesus said, "Whoever has something in his hand will receive more, and whoever has nothing will be deprived of even the little he has." (41)

Jesus said, "Blessed are the solitary and elect, for you will find the kingdom. For you are from it, and to it you will return." (49)

Jesus said, "It is I who am the light which is above them all. It is I who am the all. From me did the all come forth, and unto me did the all extend. Split a piece of wood, and I am there. Lift up the stone, and you will find me there." (77)

His disciples said to him, "When will the repose of the dead come about, and when will the new world come?" He said to them, 'What you look forward to has already come, but you do not recognize it." (51)

Lastly, the verse which has not yet been cited earlier needs a footnote.

Jesus said, "Where there are three gods, they are gods. Where there are two or one, I am with him." (30)

A translator has said of this version that it is likely "garbled" in its rendering. In another source, the two sentences which end verse 77 follow a rendering of a more complete wording of verse 30, having an additional five words that lend a much clearer meaning, regarding the "many" and the One:

Jesus said, "Where there are three, they are without God, and where there is but a single one, I say that I am with him. Lift up the stone, and you will find me there. Split the piece of wood, and I am there."

In conclusion: *"Where the beginning is, there will the end be"*; and the beginning of this Gospel declares, *"These are the secret sayings which the living Jesus spoke..."* But it becomes clear that these ancient nondual teachings were not kept secret by Jesus' predilection, but because the ruling religious authorities barred their disclosure—the "blind" and unthirsty, the "dogs" sleeping in the manger (*"Do not give what is holy to dogs, lest they throw them on the dung heap."*).

Jesus said, "Preach from your housetops that which you will hear in your ear. For no one lights a lamp and puts it under a bushel, nor does he put it in a hidden place, but rather he sets it on a lampstand so that everyone who enters and leaves will see its light." (33)

Jesus said, "The pharisees and the scribes have taken the keys of knowledge (gnosis) and hidden them. They themselves have not entered, nor have they allowed to enter those who wish to. You, however, be as wise as serpents and as innocent as doves." (39)

These enlightenment teachings are the bedrock, the requisite foundation "stones" for spiritual epiphany.

If you become my disciples and listen to my words, these stones will minister to you. (19)

Jesus said, "Show me the stone which the builders have rejected. That one is the cornerstone." (66)

Lift up the stone, and you will find me there.

Thomas said, "… a fire will come out of the stones and burn you up."

There are certain teachings of nonduality which overlap with some of the teachings that are, at least in principle, also of importance in Christianity. For example, the admonition to be, while *in* the world, not *of* the world.

But there is a theme emphasized repeatedly in the Gospel of Thomas that is found in its most consistent form nowhere in any other gospel, either canonical or apocryphal: becoming one; viewing forms as one and the same; making the two one; ending division—the ancient perspective called *nonduality*.

Elaine Pagels has stated,

> "...the cluster of sayings I take as the key to interpreting Thomas suggest that everyone, in creation, receives an innate capacity to know God....
>
> "In other words, one either discovers the light within that illuminates the whole universe or lives in darkness, within and without.
>
> "But discovering the divine light within is more than a matter of being told that it is there, for such vision *shatters one's identity...* "

The message of nonduality is that there is but *one* identity shared by "all that is." In that realization, the sense of being an "individual" self dissolves. And in that realization, the idea of the supernal, "God," being somehow *separate* and particularized dissolves.

This realization—and the recognition that this realization is the resurrection Jesus would have urged—removes the churchly garb from that awakened sage. It means that we are, by virtue of our *existence*, one with Jesus, one with God, one with all that is. And such a realization puts an end to religiosity and its benighted idea of sin and redemption, heaven and hell, Christian, Jew and Muslim.

Retired Episcopal Bishop John Shelby Spong has written:

> "Despite the enormous revolution in our understanding of immensity of space, God is still defined by these people as a supernatural being, external to the life of the world, who lives somewhere above the sky and who continues to intervene periodically in human history. The primary way that the Jesus story is still told is that he was the critical example in history of that divine intervention.

> "Traditional Christian doctrine continues to portray Jesus as a heavenly visitor who came from the God above the sky in a miraculous birth and who, when his work was complete, returned to that God by way of a cosmic flight. That completed work, says this orthodoxy, was to bring salvation to a 'fallen' world, and this was accomplished by Jesus' death on the cross.

> "On every level, each of these assertions has become for me not only literal nonsense but also little more than theological gobbledygook. Yet they are repeated in some form in the liturgies of most Christian churches every Sunday morning. I have no wish to pretend that such concepts still mean anything to me or that they are worthy of being preserved....

> "Nonetheless, I still experience life as something holy. I still believe that there is a reality, called God, that permeates all that is...."

"Many forms of religion are little more than cultural manifestations of the fear of nothingness. That is why people become hysterical when theism is challenged.

"Perhaps if we can break Jesus out of *religion*, free him from creeds, doctrines and dogmas, we can once again hear his invitation to enter the God experience *known* in the fullness of life."

The Christian church ably managed to suppress all gospels relating to Jesus' teachings other than the early contention (from at least the evangelist Paul's day forward) that the meaning of his life was relegated to a belief in the reconstitution of his dead body.

This occlusion of accounts, other than the supportive constructions of the authors of the four New Testament gospels, served its purpose for nearly two millennia.

For centuries, though, astute readers of the Bible pondered, and reflected on, the inconsistencies in the stories written by supposed "apostles" between about thirty to sixty years after the fact.

In recent times, within the past fifty to a hundred years, discoveries have begun to cast an intensifying light on the historical facts of Jesus' life and era. And the reason *why* the New Testament authors made their varying claims—and why these particular accounts were chosen to be represented as the "gospel truth"—has become discomfortingly clear.

A new religion was established, a new priestly religion, in competition with that of Judaism, the Greek and Roman polytheistic temple tributes, and the influx of spiritual perspectives from the East.

But what Jesus *taught*—which was of *real* meaning in his life—was not about founding a new religion, a church riddled with priestly mediators *between* "sinful man" and forgiving God. This *corruption* of his message was long suspected, but uncertain based on the only available "apostolic" assertions.

However, in the past sixty years, the chance discovery of nearly three dozen new—that is, previously unread—accounts of the teachings (purportedly that of Jesus) have sifted out into some rather different interpretations.

A thread running through these is that Jesus was not casting his eye skyward, dreaming of his Second Coming and those lauded disciples sitting at either hand of his throne. He had taken as his task the transmission of the experiential knowledge of one's innate divinity, the potential self-realization of one's indivisibility with the omnipresent Being that universally permeates all.

The age-old promulgation of enlightenment, by an enlightened master, evidently predated the establishment of Talmudic Judaism and Christianity. And it is a tradition whose wave was washing ashore from the East to the Near East reportedly even during Jesus' entire lifetime.

It is not surprising, then, that the treatise that focuses most exclusively on the sage's teachings—and which could possibly have been transcribed closest to the time Jesus pronounced them—is the Gospel which is least like the New Testament configuration. And so it is the contrast of this suppressed compilation which has intensified the interest of scholars to delve even more deeply into the portrayal of Jesus painted in the Bible.

Those who undertake thoroughgoing study of the New Testament, with an open mind, can come away noticeably changed.

Elaine Pagels, Ph.D., a Professor of Religion at Princeton University, authored *Beyond Belief*. While working toward her doctorate degree at Harvard, she was "astonished" to learn that there were file cabinets filled with gospels "of which I'd never heard...that [Christianity] had suppressed so effectively that only now, in the Harvard graduate school," did she learn of them.

This discovery, she said, challenged her—a Christian—"spiritually." She had already studied the writings of the church patriarch Irenaeus,

> "who had denounced such secret writings as 'an abyss of madness, and blasphemy against Christ.' Therefore I expected these recently discovered texts to be garbled, pretentious, and trivial. Instead I was surprised to find, in some of them, unexpected spiritual power..."

She carefully studied the role of Irenaeus in his influence on the formation of the theology which principally Paul had projected, particularly the Bishop's championing of the book of John for its "Christ died for our sins" evocation.

> "Only in graduate school, when I investigated each gospel, so far as possible in its historical context, did I see how radical is John's *claim* that Jesus is God manifest in human form...

> "Although John's formulations have virtually defined orthodox Christian doctrine for nearly two thousand years, they were not universally accepted in his own time.

> "What John opposed includes what the Gospel of Thomas teaches —that God's light shines not only in Jesus but, potentially at least, in everyone...."

"John says that we can experience God *only* through the divine light embodied in Jesus. But certain passages in Thomas' gospel draw a quite different conclusion: that the divine light Jesus embodied is shared by *humanity*...that the kingdom of God...is already here—*an immediate and continuing spiritual reality*...those who later enshrined the Gospel of John within the New Testament, and denounced Thomas' gospel as 'heresy,' decisively shaped—and inevitably *limited*—what would become Western Christianity."

If Thomas' gospel had not been well-known, and perhaps accepted and revered, would the author of the book of John gone to great lengths to discredit Thomas' understanding of the master?

Pagels re-read John, with scrutiny:

"John takes this teaching to mean something so different from Thomas that I wondered whether John could have written his gospel to *refute* what Thomas teaches. For *months* I investigated this possibility, and explored the work of *other* scholars who also have compared these sources; and I was finally convinced that this *is* what happened.

"As the scholar Gregory Riley points out, John—and only John—presents a challenging and *critical* portrait of the disciple he calls 'Thomas, the one called Didymus'; and, as Riley suggests, it is John who *invented* the character we call *Doubting* Thomas, perhaps as a way of caricaturing those who revered a 'teacher'—and a version of Jesus' teaching—that *he* regarded as faithless and false...

"Mark, Matthew, and Luke mention Thomas *only* as one of 'the twelve.' John singles him out as 'the doubter'—the one who failed to understand who Jesus is, or what he is saying, and rejected the testimony of the other disciples....[He] rebukes Thomas as *faithless* because he seeks to *verify* the truth *from his own experience*.

"Jesus even returns *after his death* to rebuke Thomas.... John claims in this resurrection scene (20:24-28) that Thomas had not been with the other ten, remaining disciples when Jesus had appeared earlier."

Pagels noticed:

"According to John, the meeting Thomas missed was crucial; for after Jesus greeted the ten disciples with a blessing, he formally designated *them* his apostles...

"A week later, the risen Jesus reappears and, in this climatic scene, John's Jesus rebukes Thomas for lacking faith and tells him to believe: 'Do not be faithless, but believe.' Finally Thomas, overwhelmed, capitulates and stammers out the confession, 'My Lord and my *God!*'...

"Thus John warns all his readers that they must *believe* what they cannot *verify* for themselves (namely the gospel message, to which he declares *himself* a *witness*) or face God's wrath... for here he shows Thomas *giving up* his search for *experiential truth*—his 'unbelief'...

"What John's gospel does—and has succeeded ever after in *persuading* the majority of Christians to do—is claim that only by 'believing' in Jesus can we find divine truth."

Thus Irenaeus would sanction the words of John but not of Thomas:

"Irenaeus, the Christian bishop of Lyons (c. 180), warns his flock to despise heretics who speak like this, and who 'call humankind (anthropos) the God of all things, also calling him light, and blessed, and eternal.'"

207

Another who took pains to conduct a direct study of the Bible tales was John Shelby Spong, author of *Jesus for the Non-Religious.*

Again, no stranger to the Christian catechism of "belief", he is a retired Bishop of the Episcopal Diocese of Newark, and past president of the New Jersey Council of Churches. He was a Phi Beta Kappa graduate of the University of North Carolina, and a received a Master of Divinity degree (three years later) at a theological seminary.

But religion had never been absent in his life, from the beginning:

> "I was baptized as an infant. I was confirmed as an adolescent. I was active in my church's youth group and in my university student group. I was married before the church's altar; trained at the church's seminaries, ordained deacon and priest at age 24. I served in those capacities for 21 years. I must have served well, for my church decided when I was 44 years of age that I would be elected one of its Bishops. And I was a Bishop for 24 years, retiring as the senior sitting Bishop in the Anglican Church in the United States of America. I cannot recall a time when this part of my life was not central to me."

By the nature of his career,

> "[I] immersed myself in contemporary biblical scholarship at such places as Union Theological Seminary in New York City, Yale Divinity School, Harvard Divinity School and the storied universities in Edinburgh, Oxford and Cambridge....

> "If anybody had said to me 25 years ago, [I] would wind up closer to the mystics than to any other part of the Christian tradition, I would have said, 'You got the wrong person; that's just not who I am.' But

that's who I find myself being today. And I'm quite content to allow that to take place....

"I will not shrink from allowing the scholarship of the Christian academy to dismantle piece by piece either the literalized stories of the Bible or the theological constructs that were placed on Jesus of Nazareth. I will follow where truth leads...

"Many of the things historically said about Jesus, I, as one who yearns to be a believer, can no longer hold with credibility. I need to be publicly honest about this.... I join my secular friends in renouncing them as little more than delusional ideas, in which I no longer am willing to participate."

"Humanity and divinity were not two different things that needed to be reconciled, as the church had struggled so valiantly to do in the first five hundred years of Christian history. The whole premise on which that reconciliation was postulated was simply wrong...."

"Yet clergy, trained for the most part in the academy, seem to join a conspiracy of silence to suppress this knowledge when they become pastors, fearful that if that average pew-sitter learned the content of the real debate, his or her faith would be destroyed—and with it, more importantly, his or her support for institutional Christianity...."

"What we need to embrace from this insight is that human religious systems have never been primarily a search for truth; they have always been first and foremost a search for security."

"These are the facts of existence: There is no theistic God directing these processes of cause and effect, to whom we can appeal. There is no divine plan, that we must either seek to know or await its unfolding patiently....

"The dead are not raised back into the life of this world on the fourth day after burial (in the case of Lazarus), or even on the third day (in the case of Jesus) ....

"Has it never occurred to the followers of the God-met-in-Jesus that when Jesus promised a second coming he might have been speaking not of his own mythological return, in the clouds of a theistic heaven, but rather of the *second* coming of the God who is *present* in each of us? ...

"Can we dare to embrace the possibility that we *ourselves* might be the second coming of Christ?"

And Bishop Spong knows the price of preferring historical truth to inspired truth:

"I've gotten 16 death threats in my life, but none has ever come from a Buddhist or an atheist or an agnostic; they've all come from bible-quoting true believers..."

As a similar consequence of objective New Testament study, Bart Ehrman, Ph.D., author of *Misquoting Jesus*, revised his estimation of the sanctity of "holy scripture."

Ehrman is chair of the Department of Religious Studies at the University of North Carolina at Chapel Hill. As an authority on the history of the New Testament and the historical Jesus, few equal him in expertise. In fact, few equal him in *non*-academic religious credentials.

210

As "a devoted and committed Christian," even a "born-again" and "hard-core" Christian, he could in his younger years "quote entire books of the New Testament" from memory.

He began his formal studies at Moody Bible Institute, then attended an "evangelical Christian college," and proceeded to Princeton Theological Seminary. He trained to be a minister, learned to read the gospels in their original Greek, and earned a doctorate in New Testament studies. For a year, he was pastor of a Baptist church.

The result of comparing the earliest Greek texts with their corrupted versions over time tempered his previously unquestioned faith; "my evangelical beliefs about the Bible could not hold up, in my opinion, to critical scrutiny." He concluded: "I think that if there *is* [a God], he certainly isn't the one proclaimed by the Judeo-Christian tradition…" The result: "I felt compelled to leave Christianity altogether…"

> The more I studied the manuscript tradition of the New Testament, the more I realized just how radically the text had been altered over the years at the hands of scribes, who were not only 'conserving' scripture but also *changing* it…"

> "This conviction that scribes had changed scripture became an increasing certitude for me, as I studied the text more and more."

These changes were not merely interpretations, they were conscious emendations:

> "This idea that Luke changed the text before him—in this case the Gospel of Mark—does not put him in a unique situation among the early Christian authors. This, in fact, is what all the writers of the New Testament did….

"What if both Matthew and Luke read in Mark's Gospel that Jesus became angry? Would they have been inclined to eliminate that emotion? There are, in fact, other occasions on which Jesus becomes angry in Mark. In each instance, Matthew and Luke have modified the accounts...

"We could go on nearly forever talking about specific places in which the texts of the New Testament came to be changed, either accidentally or intentionally. As I have indicated, the examples are not just in the hundreds, but in the thousands."

For example, of deliberate changes:

"Mark 1:41 originally indicated that when Jesus was approached by a leper who wanted to be healed, he became angry, reached out his hand to touch him, and said 'Be cleansed'. Scribes found it difficult to ascribe the emotion of anger to Jesus in this context, and so modified the text to say, instead, that Jesus felt compassion for the man.... the Gospels are filled with stories that have modified historical data in order to make theological points...the Gospels— whether mostly, usually, commonly, or occasionally (this is where the disputes are)—contain stories that didn't happen as told...

"I am not engaging in mere speculation that the stories about Jesus changed in the process of retelling. We have evidence that the stories were changed (or invented)...

"Moreover, these authors were not themselves eyewitnesses. They were Christians who, so far as we can tell, did not even know any eyewitnesses."

"And, in fact, we know that the original manuscripts of the Gospels did not have their authors' names attached to them...scholars continued to call these books 'Matthew, Mark, Luke, and John' as a matter of convenience...

"In fact, for half a century after the books were first put into circulation, nobody who quotes them, or even alludes to them, ever mentions their authors' names. The first time we get any inkling that a Christian knew (or cared about) who wrote these books comes from about 120–130 CE, in the writings of an obscure author named Papias...

"Apart from this tradition in Papias, we don't hear about the authors of the Gospels until near the end of the second century.

"Each of these 'authors'—as two of them actually tell us—inherited his stories from earlier written sources...

"Even more strikingly, the two leaders among Jesus' followers, Peter and John, are explicitly said in the New Testament to be 'illiterate' (Acts 4:13; the literal translation of the Greek word, sometimes given in English as 'uneducated')."

It was obvious inconsistencies such as these that led an open-minded investigator to question the soundness of blind faith in the orthodox scriptures.

The discovery of the Nag Hammadi apocrypha, and the complete Gospel of Thomas in particular, along with the subsequent focus on New Testament studies that this unearthing engendered, has lent itself to a revitalized investigation into what can be known of the sage from whose days we calculate our centuries.

213

The Jesus Seminar, convened initially in 1985, spoke of the change occurring in the attitude of academic bible scholars:

"We have too long buried our considered views of Jesus and the gospels in technical jargon and in obscure journals. We have hesitated to contradict TV evangelists and pulp religious authors for fear of political reprisal and public controversy. And we have been intimidated by promotion and tenure committees to whom the charge of popularizing or sensationalizing biblical issues is anathema. It is time for us to quit the library and speak up...

"Many Americans do not know there are four canonical gospels, and many who do can't name them. The public is poorly informed of the assured results of critical scholarship, although those results are commonly taught in colleges, universities, and seminaries. In this vacuum, drugstore books and slick magazines play on the fears and ignorance of the uniformed. Radio and TV evangelists indulge in platitudes and pieties...

"Critical scholarship is regularly under attack by conservative Christian groups. At least one Fellow of the Jesus Seminar lost his academic post as a result of his membership in the group. Others have been forced to withdraw as a consequence of institutional pressure. Latter-day inquisitors among Southern Baptist and Lutheran groups have gone witch-hunting for scholars who did not pass their litmus tests. Public attack on members of the Seminar is commonplace, coming especially from those who lack academic credentials."

The Jesus of the Gospel of Thomas would likely look with approval on changes that are nineteen hundred years overdue.

Norman Perrin has said of today's open-eyed scholars:

"It is unlikely that they will all make the same mistakes, and impossible that they should all have the same presuppositions; and in this lies our only hope for true progress."

In any case, another possibility is that an even more direct document connecting Jesus authentically to nondual enlightenment tradition may one day be unearthed in some time-forgotten location.

Perrin even went further than this cautious supposition, considering the surprises of Nag Hammadi's discovery.

"So it is theoretically possible, however practically doubtful, that we may one day have to concede that Jesus was carried to the cross, railing against God and his fate..."

Meanwhile, "keys of knowledge (gnosis)" which the pharisees "have hidden" are now unlocking some previously closed minds to true spirituality that has nothing to do with mindless religiosity.

Dear Reader,

As a coda to this book. you might like to read or listen to a short story by Robert Wolfe entitled "The Trouble Maker" which envisions the daily teaching life of Jesus.

www.karinalibrary.com/the-trouble-maker

Find an excerpt on the following page.

And, if you would like to receive updates on future Karina Library Press books and other news, you can sign up for free here:

www.karinalibrary.com/newsletter

Thoughts, feedback on this or other books or ideas for books you would like to read? Say hello at the email below.

Michael Lommel, publisher
Karina Library Press
Ojai, California

michael@karinalibrary.com

Karina Library Press: The Immensity of Life in Words, Images and Sound

FROM "THE TROUBLE MAKER"

Listeners came and went throughout the day, but a few of them sat quietly on the bare earth while he developed in greater detail the importance of personally knowing for oneself the truth of one's Divine essence—or Spirit, as the scribes called it. He recognized, among the listeners who asked relevant questions, some who had sat before him on previous visits. A few of those had even been present each day that he had spoken. It was persons such as these who followed him to Galilee, to learn what it means to translate instructive teachings into daily behavior.

He noticed warily that there was also the occasional temple officer or rabbi who passed on the fringe of the gathering, stood listening momentarily, and proceeded on. And there was sometimes at least one person sitting off to the side who appeared stiffly out of place, attempting to look studious and never smiling or laughing when the others were amused. He pretended not to be aware of these individuals, but he spoke in more traditional references in their presence, such as referring to the Eternal Kingdom rather than saying the Infinite Presence. Typically, within an hour these individuals went on about their business. ....

Read the entire story:

www.karinalibrary.com/the-trouble-maker

◎

Printed in Great Britain
by Amazon.co.uk, Ltd.,
Marston Gate.